ANSWERS TO
QUESTIONS
YOU NEVER KNEW
TO ASK

READY WRITER
Psalm 45:1

Brilliant Books Literary
137 Forest Park Lane Thomasville
North Carolina 27360 USA

CONTENTS

"BEGINNING OF THESE WRITINGS"

Isaiah 42 The Lord, who created the heavens and stretched them out, who spread out the earth and what comes from it, who gives breath to the people on it and spirit to those who walk in it. I am the Lord, I have called you in righteousness, I will take you by hand and keep you, I will give you as a covenant for the people, a light for the nations. To open the eyes that are blind, to bring out the prisoners from the dungeon, from the prison those who sit in darkness. I will lead the blind in a wat that they do not know, in paths that they have not known.

Ps 54:1 My tongue is like the pen of a ready writer.

I want to tell and talk about the Word is saying to me. For those who have an ear let them hear.

Isaiah 41:13 For I the Lord your God, hold your right hand. Isaiah 57:10 You were wearied with the length of your way, but did not say "It is hopeless", you found New Life for your strength, and so you were not faint. This I have found as the Word of Life was opening to Me. The word became new to me, opening up to teach me where I am. I ask the Lord to bring His word up to the 21st century that I might understand and apply His word to my understanding then into my walk and this is what I have found and putting together over these last nine months this book that speaks Life to me, For I had many questions but no answers, but I never stopped. For I was hungering to know for many years. Then I found a nugget and if I found one I know that there's more. That one started a new hunger and thirst for the Word of Life. I was alive but I wasn't living, barely breathing. Till a new breath of Life was breathed into me. The opening up of the infallible Word of God. Seek and keep on seeking, know and keep on knocking, ask and keep on asking. Till you find what feeds your Soul, what steers your Spirit, what is staring to satisfy your hunger, your seeking, your knocking, your asking. Then you will feel like the true bread from heaven just came out of God's oven for you. Come and dine the Lord says, enjoy Me, as I enjoy being with you.

Amos 3:3 Do two walk together unless they have agreed to meet. There are two kinds of walking and two kinds of running. We're either walking and running after the things of God, or we're walking and running after the things of the flesh.

Romans 7:5 For while we were living in the flesh, our sinful passions aroused by the law were at work n our members to bear fruit for death. 8:13 For if you live according to the flesh you will die. But if by the Spirit you put to death the deeds of the body, you will live. Ephesians 4:30 Do not grieve the Holy Spirit of God by whom you were sealed for the day of redemption. Job 32:17 The spirit within me constrains me. Ps 81:13 Oh that my people would listen to Me and walk in my ways. Galatians 5:11 For the desires for the flesh are against the Spirit and the desires of the Spirit are against the flesh. For these are opposed to each other, to keep you from doing the things you want to do.

How to start this book. Through prayer, asking, and seeking knowledge. Through wanting to know if a deeper walk in the Word will end in understanding being revealed? I prayed and asked the Lord to bring His Word that is the same yesterday, today, and forever. To bring it up to the 21st century for my understanding. Starting from 2000-4000 years ago to open the eternal Word to my understanding and how His Word speaks to me. That understanding may come forth that will give me insight from his Word that I may grow thereby.

That understanding comes first, to me, then others as God wills. God's Word is active, alive, and will do what it says it will do. Looking at the life of Jesus and receiving understanding is my heart's desire. If you put ten people in a room and in the room there is one big diamond, and the ten people stand around that one diamond and that diamond is Jesus, all are given an assignment to write down what they see. You might get ten different perspectives of their view: Its shape, clarity, cut, depth, and beauty. I wonder and wish that it were mine. Ten different views, ten different insights, are all describing what they see.

What is seen in the diamond represents Jesus. Ten may see Him in a different way, a different light, but it's all Him. Now, talk among yourselves and go and tell the world what you have discovered that's been hidden from the foundation of the world. To whom much is given, much is required. Life comes from speaking life. Blessed are your eyes, for now you see. Blessed are your ears, for now you hear. What we see now and what we hear, we're to tell, for the benefit of those who are deaf and blind that they may receive sight and hearing into the Word of life. "I once was lost, but now I'm found, blind but now I see."

God's Word brings life to the dead, hearing to the deaf, and restores sight to the blind. Even though we may have 20/20 vision, without Christ we're all blind. So blind that we cannot see heavenly things, and we will miss heaven even though it's right before us. "But blessed are those who have eyes to see and ears to hear the Word of eternal life, now and into eternity."

I am going to try and pen what I see from God's Word how this diamond, Jesus, speaks to me in my walk. You may receive something, or I pray you won't reject what I'm saying. Cars have seat belts, trucks have seat belts, and roller coasters fasten you in, so get ready for perhaps the ride of your life.

"But the Lord said to me, do no say I am only a youth, for to all to whom I send you, you shall go, and whatsoever I command you, you shall speak."

The parable of the Good Samaritan, from the book of Luke 10:30-34

Please allow me to introduce myself. I am the Good Samaritan about whom Jesus tells this parable in the book of Luke, 10:30-34. Let me tell you something about myself. I did not know what a Christian was. I never heard about being born again, or that I could be forgiven of my sin, until my sister came back home one day after going to Jacob's well to draw water. She told me and others that she had met the Christ at the well. She said that He told her everything that she had done, that He knew that she had been married five times, and that the man she was living with was not her husband. He knew her husbands by name and told her about them. He told her he was the Christ, and that she was one of the first to know.

He said, no longer do we worship at Jerusalem or in this mountain; that worship comes from the heart, no longer from temples and mountains. It is in the spirit and truth of Christ that she can be forgiven of her sins. Jesus left Jacob's well and came to Sychar and stayed two days. Many Samaritans from the town believed in Him because of my sister's testimony. Many more believed because of His words, for we have heard for ourselves, and we know that this indeed is the Savior of the world. I, myself, believed that day and was saved, forgiven, set free. I did not even know what I needed to be set free from, but I knew it and I felt it. I'm here in Jerusalem these last couple days, sharing the truth about Christ. This afternoon I'm going down to Jericho and preach the truth of Christ to those who have ears to hear. But first, I'm going over to the city gate, where more people will be gathering together to share what truth I know with them before I leave to go to Jericho.

As the Lord said to Jeremiah in 17:19, "The Lord said to me, 'Go and stand in the peoples' gate, by which the kings of Judah enter and by which they go out, and in all the gates of Jerusalem, and say: Hear the word of the Lord, you kings of Judah, and all Judah, and all the inhabitants of

Jerusalem who enter by these gates. O hear, all you citizens of Jerusalem, the word from the Lord.'"

LUKE 13:34

"Jesus himself said, 'O, Jerusalem, Jerusalem, the city that kills the prophets and stones those who are sent to it, How often would I have gathered your children together as a hen gathers her brood under her wings, and you were not willing?'"

2 Cor 3:3: "We are a letter from Christ, written not with ink but with the spirit of the living God, not on tablets of stone but on the tablets of our hearts,"

2 Cor 12:1: "Therefore I talk, that I might go on to visions and revelation of the Lord."

2 Cor 11:6: "Even if I am unskilled in speaking, I am not so in knowledge."

2 Cor 4:13: "I believe, and so I speak."

2 Cor 12:9: "That His grace is sufficient for me, for my power is made perfect in weakness. Therefore, I will boast all the more gladly of my weakness, so that the power of Christ may rest upon me."

Eph 3:3-5: "The mystery was made known to me by revelation. When you hear me speak, you can perceive my insight into the mystery of Christ, which now has been revealed to His holy apostles and prophets by the Spirit."

Eph 1:17: "Which now can be revealed to any who believe that the God of our Lord Jesus Christ, the Father of glory may give to you the spirit of wisdom and revelation in the knowledge of Him."

Gal 6:8: "The one who sows to the Spirit will from the Spirit reap eternal life."

2 Cor 4:16: "So I do not lose heart, though our outward self is wasting away, my inner self is being renewed day by day."

Gal 4:16: "Therefore have I become your enemy because I tell you the truth?"

2 Cor 5:10: "For we must all appear before the judgment seat of Christ so that each one may receive what is due for what he has done in the body, whether good or evil."

Rom 15:18: "Allow me to say this and hear me well. You that have gathered here today, for I will not venture to speak of anything except what Christ has accomplished through me to bring those who hear me to the obedience by word and deed."

Oh people of Jerusalem who have gathered here, what I say to one I say to all. Be mindful of the words which were spoken before by the prophets and of the commandments of the apostle of the Lord Jesus Christ. I say not these things to shame you, my people, I warn you. Know you not that your body is the temple of the Holy Ghost, which you have of God, and you are not your own? For you were bought with a price, therefore glorify God in your body and in your spirit, which are God's. In all things showing yourself a pattern of good works and doctrine, showing uncorruptness, gravity, sincerely sound speech that cannot be condemned. That He, that is of the contrary part, may be ashamed for having no evil thing to say of you. A good name is rather to be chosen than riches, for He is the Lord, which has separated you from other people. Wherein, they think it strange that you run not with them to the same excess of riot, speaking evil of you. Be you therefore sober and watch unto prayer. If any man speaks, let him speak as the oracles of God. If any man minister, let him do it as the ability which God gives, for the thought of foolishness is sin. You adulterers and adulteresses, know you not that the friendship of the world is enemy with God? Whosoever therefore will be a friend of the world is the enemy of God.

Be not deceived. Evil communication corrupts good manners, and a whisper separates good friends. So, grieve not the holy spirit of God, whereby you are sealed until the day of redemption. Yes, we are to reprove, rebuke, exhort with all long-suffering and doctrine. For the wicked shall fall by his own wickedness. Who has said, with our tongue we will prevail? Our lips are our own, who is the Lord over us? And having a heart that devises wicked imagination, feet that be swift to run to mischief, and none call for justice, nor any plead for truth. Deliver me from all my transgressions, make me not the reproach of the foolish. But He that regards reproof shall be honored. If sinners entice you, consent not. For we must present our bodies a living sacrifice, wholly acceptable to God, which is our reasonable service. For we are epistles known and read of all men and if we be reproached for the name of Christ, happy are we. Amen.

Rom 15:18: "For I will not venture to speak of anything except what Christ has accomplished through me."

Proverbs 1:20

O people of Jerusalem. To know wisdom and instruction, to receive instruction in wise dealings. Fools despise wisdom, wisdom cries aloud in the streets.

Wisdom raises her voice, wisdom cries out – how long, you simple ones, love being simple and fools hate knowledge? For I will make My words known to you. I have called, and you refuse to listen. I've stretched out My hand, and no one has heeded. You have ignored all My counsel and reproof. I will laugh at your calamity, mock when terror strikes you. When you call upon Me, I will not answer. You will seek Me, but will not find Me, because you hate knowledge and did not choose the fear of the Lord. You shall eat the fruit of your own way, but if you listen to Me, you will dwell secure and will be at ease. Make your ear attentive to wisdom, that you will understand righteousness, for wisdom will come into your heart so you will be delivered from the forbidden woman, from the adulteress with her smooth words, for none who go into her come back.

Nor do they regard the path of life, for He has said, "My son, do not forget my teachings, for length of day and years of life they will add to you. Then you will find favor and good success in the sight of God and man. Your barns will be filled with plenty, for My wisdom is more precious than jewels. Nothing you desire can compare with her. She is a tree of life to those who lay hold of her. Then your foot will not slip. The Lord will be your confidence to the humble He gives favor. The wise will inherit honor. Get wisdom, get insight. Do not turn away from the words of My mouth. Do not forsake her, she will keep you when you walk, your steps will not be hampered. Keep hold of instruction, for she is life."

Be attentive to my words, for they are life to those who find them. Ponder the path of your feet, then all your ways will be sure. My son, keep your Father's commandments. He who commits adultery lacks sense. Keep My words, and treasure up My commandments with you. For I love those who love Me. Those who seek Me, find Me.

For there is an inheritance to those who love Me, and blessed is the one who listens to Me. Give instructions to a wise man and he will become still wiser. The Lord does not let the righteousness go hungry, for blessings are on the head of the righteous. The wise of heart will receive commandments. The mouth of the righteous is a fountain of life, on the lips of him who has understanding, wisdom is found.

For whosoever heeds instruction is on the path of life. The fear of the Lord prolongs life. The integrity of the upright guides them. The righteousness of the upright delivers them.

Where there is no guidance, people fall. A man who is kind benefits himself. For whosoever is steadfast in righteousness will live. And one gives freely, yet grows all the richer. Another withholds what he should give, and only suffers want. The people curse him who holds back grain. The fruit of the righteous is the tree of life. For whosoever loves discipline loves knowledge. No one is established by wickedness.

For whosoever works his land will have plenty of bread. The way of a fool is right in his own eyes, and anxiety in a man's heart weighs him down. In the paths of righteousness is life, and in its pathway there is no death. The light of the righteous rejoice, but the lamp of the wicked will be put out. Poverty and disgrace comes to him who ignores instructions.

For whosoever walks with the wise becomes wise. The one who is wise is cautious and turns away from evil. The fear of the Lord is a fountain of life. The lips of the wise spread knowledge, for there is severe discipline for him who forsakes the way. He will not go to the wise. For folly is joy to him who lacks sense. The thoughts of the wicked are an abomination. Wisdom and humility come before honor. And whosoever guards his way preserves his life. Whosoever gives thought to the Word will discover good.

For good sense is a fountain of life to him who has it. Why should a fool have money in his hand to buy wisdom when he has no sense? For a joyful heart is good medicine. You know to impose a fine on a righteous man is not good, nor to strike a noble for their righteousness. But whosoever isolates himself seeks his own desire. For who can say, I have made my heart pure? The lips of knowledge are a precious jewel.

For the lamp will be put out in utter darkness, for the one who curses his father and mother. Do not say, I will repay evil. Wait for the Lord, and He will deliver you. When a scoffer is punished, the simple become wise. For the one who wanders from the way of good sense will remain in the assembly of the dead. The reward of humility and fear of the Lord is riches and honor and life. It is the glory of God to conceal things, but the glory of kings to search them out.

Iron sharpens iron, and one man sharpens another. If one turns away his ear from hearing the law, even his prayer will be an abomination. To show partiality is not good. He who is often reproved, yet stiffens his neck, will suddenly be broken beyond hearing. For every word of God proves true.

The Lord has said, 'When I called you did not answer. When I spoke, you did not listen, but you did what was evil in My eyes and chose what I did not delight in.'

Isa 42:6-8: "For He said, I am the Lord. I have called you in righteousness. I will take you by the hand and keep you, I will give you as a covenant for the people, a light for the nations. To open the eyes that are blind, to bring out the prisoners from the dungeon, from the prison those who sit in darkness. I am the Lord, that is My name. He who has an ear, let him hear what the Spirit says."

1 Cor 3:5: "Let him become a fool that he may become wise." That's a fool for Christ which is foolish to our thinking and the ways of this world. Just faith in Christ alone is foolishness to the thinking of this world.

Rom 8:7: "For the mind that is set on the flesh is hostile to God, for it does not submit to God's law. Indeed, it cannot."

2 Cor 3-5: "Not that I am sufficient in myself to claim anything as coming from me, but my sufficiency is from God, who has made me sufficient by the Spirit that gives life. Such is the confidence that I have through Christ. Not to talk about the letter of the law, but of the Spirit that gives life. For the ministry of death, carved in stone, came with such glory which was being brought to an end. How much more the ministry of the Spirit can have even more glory? For that which was being brought to an end came with glory. How much more will what is permanent have glory? This in itself gives me the boldness in this new life, because only through Christ is it taken away. When one turns to the Lord, the veil is removed. Where the Spirit is, there is freedom. We do not lose heart. The god of this world has blinded the minds of the unbelievers to keep them from seeing the light of the Gospel of the glory of Christ. His light has shone out of the darkness, has shone in my heart. To give the light of knowledge of the glory of God in the face of Jesus Christ. That the surpassing power belongs to God and not to myself. Knowing that, He who raised Christ will also raise us. So do not lose heart. For we walk by faith, not by sight. For we will all appear before the judgment seat of Christ, so that each one will receive what is due, for what he has done in the body, whether good or bad. Therefore, if anyone is in Christ, he is a new creation and all things become new. For our sake Jesus was made sin for us, who knew no sin. That in Him we become the righteousness of God. And that is why I am here today, not for me but for you."

Rom 8:11-12: "Behold the days are coming, declares the Lord God, when I will send a famine on the land; not a famine of bread, nor a thirst for water, but of hearing the word of the Lord."

Ps 118:22: "For the stone which the builder rejected has become the chief cornerstone."

Acts 4:11: "This Jesus is the stone, which was despised and rejected by you, the builders. But which has become the head of the corner, the cornerstone. There is salvation in and through no one else. For there is no other name under heaven given among men by which we must be saved, Jesus, who was crucified."

Jer 18:11-12: "Return, everyone, from his evil ways, and amend your ways and your deeds. But they say that is in vain! We will follow our own plans, and will every one act according to the stubbornness of his evil heart! As the Lord told Jeremiah, 'Go and stand in the peoples' gates.' Take care for the sake of your lives. But they said, 'Come, let us strike him with the tongue and let us not pay attention to any of his words.'"

My prayer is that what was said here today will pierce your hearts with understanding, open your eyes to the truth of Christ and why He came. I am leaving now and going down to Jericho. You that believe, please pray for the message that the will of the Lord be done, and thank you all.

I would like to say something about this man that left Jerusalem and fell among thieves. I believe that he was saved, somewhat a new believer, a new convert to Christ. Sharing his testimony, this man was witnessing about what he knew about Jesus Christ; that He was his Savior, and how he was forgiven of his sins and that this life in Christ is real and he was rejoicing in this newfound life. This man had left Jerusalem just ahead of me, for he was going down to Jericho.

Now there were men in Jerusalem who did not like what they were hearing from this man, and wanted to put an end to his belief in Christ and silence his witness and the spreading of the Gospel of Jesus Christ.

So as this man was going down to Jericho, he fell among robbers who stripped him of his clothing. They beat him and departed, leaving him half-dead. Now by chance a priest was going down that road, and when he saw him, he passed by on the other side.

Phil 2:21: "For they seek their own interests, not those of Jesus Christ."

Now this man was not beaten up. He still had his robe on, shoes on, no blood, no bruises. He was not touched in any way physically, and was leaning up against a rock, sitting in the shade, in disbelief of what had just happened to him. The man's beating took place in his heart, at the Spirit of the matter – where life proceeds from.

Obad 1:7: "Those at peace with you have deceived you, they have prevailed against you, they have set a trap for you."

This man was set up. His fall was planned.

Hos 6:9: "As robbers lie in wait for a man, so the priests banded together. They murder on the way to Shechem, they commit villainy. The wicked lie in wait to destroy me. They heard my testimony and are out to destroy my testimony along with me."

Prov 1:11: "If they say, come with us, let us lie in wait for blood, let us ambush the innocent without reason."

Ps 56:6: "They stir up strife, they lurk, they watch my steps as they have waited for my life."

Deut 31:9: "Moses wrote this law and gave it to the priests and the sons of Levi who carried the ark of the covenant of the Lord, and to all the elders of Israel."

It's one thing to be physical with the things of God, and another to be spiritual, connected, and involved. We can act out things, be busy about the things of God, and miss out on the Spirit of the movement of God, therefore justifying ourselves, and missing the true direction of God.

The priest and the Levite did not see the spiritual need. Their eyes had not been opened or illuminated to the spiritual need of this man. Therefore, they were blind!

Rom 8:7: "The carnal mind is enmity against God, for it is not subject to the law of God; neither indeed can it be."

Prov 21:13: "Whoever closes his ear to the cry of the poor will himself call out and not be answered."

Now this man cries out to the Lord for mercy and help. For being so naïve and in not seeing their plan for his destruction, with their lying words that deceive men.

Ps 142:1-7: "With my voice I cry out to the Lord, with my voice I plead for mercy to the Lord. I pour out my complaint before Him, I tell my trouble before Him. When my spirit faints within me, You know my way. In the path where I walk they have hidden a trap for me. Look to the right and see, there is none who takes notice of me. No refuge remains to me, no one cares for my soul. I cry to you, O Lord, I say, You are my refuge, my portion in the land of the living. Attend to my cry, for I am brought very low! Deliver me from my persecutors, for they are too strong for me! Bring me out of prison, that I may give thanks to your Name! The righteous will surround me, for you will deal bountifully with me."

Ps 5:1-12: "Give ear to my words, O Lord, consider my groaning. Give attention to the sound of my cry. To You do I pray."

Ps 18:6: "In my distress I called upon the Lord. To my God I cried for help."

Ps 143:1-2: "Hear my prayer, O Lord, give ear to my pleas for mercy! In Your faithfulness answer me, in Your righteousness! For the enemy has pursued my soul, he has crushed my life to the ground, he has made me sit in darkness like those long dead. Therefore, my spirit faints within me. I meditate on all that You have done, I ponder the work of Your hands. O, Lord, I stretch out my hands to You, my soul thirst for You like a parched land. O answer me quickly, O Lord! My spirit fails! Hide not Your face from me, lest I be like those who go down to the pit. I life up my soul, let me hear of Your steadfast love, for in You I trust. Make me know the way I should go, for to You I lift up my soul. Deliver me from my enemies, Lord! I have fled to You for refuge. Teach me to do your will, for You are my God. For Your name's sake, O Lord, preserve my life! In your righteousness bring my soul out of trouble! And in Your steadfast love You will cut off my enemies, and You will destroy all the adversaries of my soul, for I am Your servant."

Ps 28:1: "To you, O Lord, I call my rock, be not deaf to me."

Ps 17:5: "My steps had held fast to Your paths, my feet have not slipped."

Ps 19:14: "Oh let the words of my mouth, and the meditation of my heart, be acceptable in Your sight, O Lord, my rock and my redeemer."

Ps 37:32: "The wicked watch for the righteous and seek to put him to death."

Ps 119:95: "The wicked they lie in wait to destroy me."

Ps 140:4: "O Lord my God, guard me from the hands of the wicked, preserve me from violent men who have planned to trip up my feet."

Jer 9:8: "Their tongue is a deadly arrow, it speaks deceitfully. With their mouth they speak peace, but in his heart he plans an ambush for me."

Ps 64:2: "Hide me, Lord, from the secret plots of the wicked, from the evildoers."

Ps 141:1: "O give ear to my voice when I call, let my prayer be counted as incense before You. O Lord, let a righteous man strike me, let him rebuke me, for it is oil for my head."

Ps 141:9-10: "Keep me from the trap that they have laid for me, let Your Spirit lead me."

Ps 119:49-50: "Remember Your word to Your servant in which You have made me hope. This is my comfort in my affliction that Your promise gives me life."

Ps 31:22: "You have heard the voice of my pleas for mercy when I cried to You for help."

Ps 32:7: "You are a hiding place for me."

Ps 32:10: "You have said that steadfast love surrounds the one who trusts in You, Lord."

Ps 139:15-16: "That my frame was not hidden from You, when I was being made in secret. Your eyes saw my unformed substance; in Your book were written every one of them, when as yet there were none of them."

Ps 27:1: "O Lord, be not far from me."

Lam 3:56: "You hear my plea, do not close Your ear to my cry for help!"

Ps 118:5: "Out of my distress I called on You, Lord. Answer me and set me free."

Ps 37:12: "For the wicked have plots against me and gnashed their teeth at me."

Ps 17:5: "My steps have held fast to Your paths, my feet have not slipped."

Ps 139:23-24: "Search me, O God, and know my heart. Try me and know my thoughts, and see if there be any wicked way in me."

Ps 119:92-93: "For if Your law had not been my delight I would have perished in my affliction. I will never forget Your precepts, for by them You have given me life."

Ps 19:3: "For Lord, I know that there is no speech, nor are there words, whose voice is not heard by You."

Ps 121:1: "I lift up my eyes to the hills, from where does my help come."

Isa 40:31: "For they who wait upon the Lord shall renew their strength."

Ps 25:15: "O Lord my God, You will pluck my feet out of the net they have spread for me."

Ps 119:110: "The wicked have laid a snare for me, but I do not stray from Your precepts."

Mic 7:7: "I will look to the Lord, I will wait for the God of my salvation, my God will hear me."

Ps 9:9: "You, Lord, are my stronghold in the time of trouble."

Ps 63:8: "To you, Lord, my soul clings."

Ps 145:18: "For Lord, You have said that You are near to all who call upon You, those who call on Him in truth."

Ps 147:3: "He heals the brokenhearted and binds up their wounds.:

Ps 16:11: "Lord, You make known to me the path of life. O help me now."

Ps 119:159: "O Lord my God, give me life according to your steadfast love."

Ps 119:28: "For You are my God, and I will give thanks to You."

Ps 56:13: "For You have delivered my soul from death, yes, my feet from falling, that I may walk before God in the light of life."

Ps 119:10: "For with my whole heart I seek You."

Ps 119:77-78: "Oh Lord, let Your mercy come to me, that I may live. For Your law is my delight. Let the insolent be put to shame, because they have wronged me with falsehood."

Ps 119:105: "For Lord, Your word is a lamp to my feet and a light to my path."

Ps 123:1: "To You I lift up my eyes."

Ps 7:8: "O Lord, according to my righteousness and according to the integrity that is in me."

Ps 27:9: "Hide not Your face from me, turn not Your servant away, You who have been my help."

Ps 143:1: "O Lord, hear my prayer, give ear to my pleas for mercy."

Ps 40:4: "For blessed is the man who makes the Lord his trust."

Jer 33:3: "In the book of Jeremiah, Lord, you have said, 'Call upon Me and I will answer you.'"

Ps 25:2: "O my God, I trust in You, let me not be ashamed, let not mine enemies triumph over me."

Ps 119:92-93: "For if Your law had not been my delight, I would have perished in my affliction. Yes, God, send help, for I will never forget Your precepts, for by them You have given me life."

Ps 102:17: "For You, God, regard the prayer of the destitute and do no despise their prayer."

Ps 55:2: "Attend to me."

Ps 55:4-6: "For my heart is in anguish within me, the terrors of death have fallen upon me. Fear and trembling come upon me. I say, Oh, that I had wings like a dove I would fly away and be at rest."

Ps 51:17: "For the sacrifices of God are a broken spirit, a broken heart, O God, you will not despise."

Ps 119:71: "It is good for me that I was afflicted, that I might learn Your statutes."

Ps 119:77: "O Lord, let mercy come to me, that I may live."

In the story of the good Samaritan, the priest and the Levite both saw him and both passed by, one on one side and one on the other side. The priest and the Levite could not see the problem-they needed to be saved themselves. Both were spiritually blind - religious, blind guides.

Rom 14:12: "Each of us will give an account of himself to God."

But the Samaritan came to where he was, and when he saw him, he had compassion. Why? Because the Good Samaritan saw the true problem. **Acts 14:9:** "Keep me from the trap that they have laid for me and from the snares of evildoers!"

Jer 9:8: "Their tongue is a deadly arrow. It speaks deceitfully; with their mouth each speaks peace to his neighbor, but in his heart he plans an ambush for me."

These men wanted to rob him, strip him of his testimony. They thought what he believed was all lies and that there was no such thing as salvation or being born again. Who is going to believe that stuff anyway? No church would accept you through their doors, give it up, and away they went.

Now the Good Samaritan poured oil and wine on the man's sores.

Prov 21:20: "Precious treasure and oil are in a wise man's dwelling."

Oil and wine came out from the spirit, the heart of the Good Samaritan and off his tongue. The words of life went into this man's ear and down into his broken spirit. Then healing took place, deliverance from a broken and contrite spirit, with life restored to the man.

Prov 10:21: "The lips of the righteous feed man."

Then the Good Samaritan took him to an inn, and there they shared the light of the truth till early morning. With all expenses paid in full by one faithful brother!

AMEN!

EYE HAS NOT SEEN 1 CORINTHIANS 2:9

Eye has not seen, nor ear heard, the things that God has for those who love Him.

I'm not saying that what you're about to read is 100 percent true or even 100 percent real.

I just want to pin down what the Word says to me. I want to encourage you by my walk in the Lord.

The scripture says, "Seek and you'll find, knock and the door will be open."

I never want to stop seeking, to stop asking, to stop knocking for it is an unending book, and in this life, we will never come to know it all.

We are to live and move and have our being in the Word of life.

So, what the Word is saying is that we can live in that Word, we can move in that Word, and we can have our being in that Word.

Understanding can come to each one of us in the place in Christ where we have obtained.

That's what we walk in, where we have obtained, where we have matured.

To help others, and for others to help us.

What word of life did we read that stirred our spirit, that put a smile on our face? Where we found a word of encouragement, without using a concordance, without the Matthew Henry Commentary. Just one on one with the word, and the word being revealed to us.

The book Pilgrims Progress, by John Bunyan, was written from a prison in 1678 with no concordance, no commentaries.

Just John Bunyan and the Spirit and his recall of what he had read and held onto in his life, causing him to pen the book Pilgrims Progress.

Who corrected him?

Who said that's wrong, John?

You shouldn't have written that.

I've heard that it's the next best book to read after the Bible.

I've read it twice.

Because of other men, I've held back in my writings, with my conversation in the word when I didn't know enough to write anything down. But I am where I am, and I'm writing from where I am.

I know not any whose walk in the Lord is identical.

That's why iron sharpens iron.

That we need each other's countenance, each other's correction, each other's direction.

One another's wisdom from the Word of life.

Amen.

GOD FORMED MAN FROM THE DUST FROM THE GROUND

Genesis 2:7, "Then the Lord God formed the man of Dust from the ground and breathed into his nostrils the Breath of Life, and the man became a living creature." Genesis 3:19, "By the sweat of your face you shall eat bread, till you return to the Ground for out of it You Were Taken, for you are Dust, and to Dust you shall return." Ecclesiastes 3:20, "All go to one place. All are from the Dust, and to Dust all return." Ps 103:14, "For He knows our frame, He remembers that we are Dust." Ecclesiastes 12:7, "The Dust returns to the earth as it was, and the Spirit returns to God who gave it." Job 20:11, "His bones are full of his youthful vigor, but it Will lie down with him in the Dust."

"MATTHEW 25:1, 13"

Then the kingdom of heaven will be like ten virgins who took their lamps and when to meet the bridegroom. Five of them were foolish, and five were wise. When the foolish took their lamps, they took no oil with them, but the wise took oil with their lamps. As the bridegroom was delaying, they all became drowsy and slept. But at midnight there was a cry, here is the bridegroom, come out to meet him. Then all those virgins arose and trimmed their lamps. And the foolish said to the wise, give us some of your oil, for our lamps are going out. But the wise answered there will not be enough for us and for you. "Go rather to those who sell and buy for yourselves, while they were going to buy the bridegroom came, and those who" were ready went in with him to the marriage feast and the door was SHUT.

Where were the five foolish virgins going, they never ask the wise where do we go, who is selling, what do we buy, and what do we buy it with? The five foolish virgins never asked these questions, because they knew where to go, and who was selling what they needed, and what the price was to purchase what they were lacking. They knew but now it was too late the door was SHUT, in a twinkling of an eye it was finish. Through there walk with Christ they squandered it away, let it slip through their hands.

In a way the world had become more inviting, thus becoming a fool in this parable. Who was selling what they needed? The person selling what they needed they knew. The true pastors of God handing out the true of God's word.

Isaiah 55:1: Come All You Who are thirsty, come to the waters, and you who have no money, come, buy, and eat. Come buy wine and milk without money and without cost. The Economy of God is our faith! We're sitting in church, hearing the word the revelation of his word. When we agree with the truth, just slightly nod of are head in agreement to the truth we just bought IT! When the five foolish virgins went to buy, the true pastures were raptured out along with the five wise, and the door was SHUT, truth was nowhere to be had. When the five foolish virgins came back and knocking at the door, the Lord did not say come in. He said depart from me, for I never "knew you". Now God knows everybody, even from the womb he fashioned us. When God said, "I never knew you," what he was saying was, I never knew you IN ME! All ten were saved, born again, and have accepted Christ. Ten virgins, all having their wedding garment, spotless gowns ready to meet the Lord. All having lamps filled with oil and lit. Before I was saved I never had a gown, I wasn't a virgin in God's eyes, I had no lamp, no oil, and I wasn't lit. Until after I receive Jesus Christ as my savior, becoming His bride that he clothed me with my garment of Salvation and gave me a new name and a lamp that burns. Now do not forsake Me. AMEN

"MORE ON MATT 25, THE 10 VIRGINS"

II Samuel 22:29: For you are my lamp oh Lord, and the Lord will lighten my darkness.

Psalm 18:28: You Lord keep my lamp burning, my God turns my darkness into light.

Ps 119:105: Your word is a lamp unto my feet, and a light unto my path.

Leviticus 24: The Lord said unto Moses, commanding the children of Israel that they bring pure oil for the light, to cause the lamp to burn continually, it shall be a statue forever in your Generations.

Galatians 3:1: Oh foolish Galatians who has Bewitched you that you should not obey the truth.

Ecc 9:8: Let your garments be always White, and let your head lack no ointment

Isa 62:1: For Zion's sake, Will I not hold my peace, and for Jerusalem sake, will not rest, until the righteousness thereof go forth as brightness, the salvation thereof as a lamp that burns.

Prov 21:20: There is treasure to be desired and oil in the dwelling of the wise, but a foolish man spins it up.

Prov 10:21: The lips of the righteous feed many, but fools die for wand of wisdom.

Prov 10 :11: The mouth of righteous man is a well of life.

Prov 10:13: And the lips of him that has understanding wisdom is found.

I Tim 4:15: Meditate up on these things, give yourself to them, that you're profiting may appear to all.

II Peter 3:10: The day of the Lord will come as a thief in the night. but go to them that sell, and buy for yourselves.

Prov 23:23: By the truth and sell it not, also wisdom, and instruction, and understanding. While they went to buy the bridegroom came.

Isa 55:1: Everyone that thirst, come to the waters, and he that has no money, come and buy and eat, come buy wine and milk. "God says, I'll feed the hungry resist the proud."

II Chronicles 7:14: If my people which are called by my name, shall humble Themselves, and pray, and seek my face, and turn from their wicked ways. Then will I hear from heaven, and will forgive their sin, and will heal their land.

'JOHN 8:1-11 THE WOMAN CAUGHT IN ADULTERY'

Number one, why did not the priest bring the man who was caught in adultery with the woman. But brought only the women. The Law said that both should be stoned, anyone caught in adultery. They wanted the Law upheld why not all the way. The Priest said to Jesus, what do you say. Setting a trap for Jesus with his words. Then Jesus stooped down and was writing on the ground. Then saying he who is without sin, you cast the first stone. Then they drooped their stones, from the oldest to the youngest, and left. What came to me was. Jesus wrote in the sand. 'All of you have had her' and they drooped their stones and left. From the oldest to the youngest. Maybe the younger seeing the older or those that were above him drop their stones, so the younger followed. I thought that the older went first in dropping their stone because they themselves had more sin then the younger. The conviction of their lives caused them to drop there stones. Looking for another opportunity to falsely accuse Jesus. They had been caught by the Spirits conviction. "Reason for stoning." Stone the women she won't tell or talk to anybody about us now." Like David and Uriah David had Uriah killed to cover up his sin didn't work. AMEN.

MANNA AND QUAIL

Exodus 16: On the fifteenth day of the second month after coming out of Egypt. The whole congregation of the people of Israel Grumbled against Moses and Aaron in the wilderness. It would have been better that we had died by the hand of the Lord in the land of Egypt, when we sat by the meat pots and ate bread to our full. For you have brought us out into this wilderness to kill this whole assembly with hunger. The Lord said to Moses, "Behold I am about to rain bread from Heaven for you. The people shall go out and gather a day's portion every day, that I may 'test them' to see if they will walk in My law or not. On the sixth day they will bring in twice as much as they gather daily. In the morning dew lay around the camp. When the dew had gone up, a fine flake like thing, fine as frost on the ground." The people said what is it. Moses said it is the "Bread that the Lord has given you to eat." Take an Omer, according to the number of the persons that each of you has in "his tent." Each of them gathered as much as he" could eat and Moses said to them. Let no one leave any of it over till the morning. But they did not listen to Moses. Some left part of it till the morning and it had worms and stank.

They were to gather morning by morning, but on the sixth day they gather twice as much bread. They laid it aside until morning and it "did not stink, and there were no worms I it." Eat today for you will not find it in the field. But on the seventh day "some went out to gather, but they found none." Now the house of Israel called its name Manna. The people of Israel ate Manna forty years, until they came to habitable land, to the border of the land of Canaan.

Numbers 11: And the people complained in the hearing of the Lord. "Oh that we had meat to eat! We Remember the fish we ate in Egypt that cost nothing, the cucumbers, the melons, the leeks the onions and the garlic. But now there is nothing at all but this Manna to look at." Moses said to the people. Consecrate yourselves for tomorrow and you shall eat Meat, for the Lord heard you say, "Who will give us meat to eat?" For it was Better for us in Egypt," therefor the Lord will give you meat, and you shall eat. You shall not eat just ONE day or TWO days or FIVE days or TEN days or TWENTY days, But the WHOLE MONTH, until it comes out your nostrils and becomes loathsome to you, because you have rejected the Lord who is among you and have wept before Him, saying, "Why did we come out of Egypt?"

About seventy-five days after coming out of Egypt the people started their Grumbling. It would have been better if we would have died in the hand of the Lord in Egypt, when we sat by the meat pots and ate bread to the full. The people if Israel set free from their bondage, slavery, Pharaoh, their task masters, gathering their own straw to make bricks. Within seventy-five days of being set free seeing the miracles of God, and now wanting to go Back to their task master, slavery and bondage. Now, today, why did I ever get Saved anyway, this is not fun. I've lost all my old friends. If I had just a drink I would feel much better, the life I left behind wasn't so bad now.

Then the Lord said to Moses. I am about to rain Bread from Heaven for you, and the people they shall go out and gather a day's portion every day, that I may "test them" whether they will do what I say or not. On the sixth day when they prepare what they bring in, it will be twice as much as they gather daily.

Today Jesus is the BREAD THAT CAME DOWN FROM HEAVEN. We who have been Set Free from our Sins and Life of bondage "Are to pick up daily, the word of God, the True Bread from Heaven, that will not gather worms, nor stink as they were tested in the wilderness, will they obey, so we are tested.

The Spirit lives within us, and we need to feed the Spirit daily, as much as we can take in and no more, from the word of God. His Manna His Bread to feed His Spirit He gave us the day that we got Saved. Until we grow into the full statue of what He has called us to be. Line upon line, precept upon precept. Gathering of the word of God, our daily BREAD that sustains us, our daily portion of Spiritual survival.

Rev 2:17: I will give some of the hidden Manna. Hidden Manna God's revealed word, God's revelation.

What are we feeding on, that is what we will become, and what we are feeding on goes not in our mouth

Matt 13:35: I will open my mouth in parables, I will utter what has been hidden since the foundation of the world.

John 4:32: I have food to eat that you do not know about.

Prov 18:20: From the fruit of a man;s mouth his stomach is satisfied. "From the fruit of the Spirit the man's spiritual stomach is satisfied.

John 6:33: For the bread of God is He who came down from Heaven and gave Life to the world. V 35 I am the Bread of Life, whoever comes to Me shall not hunger, and whoever believes in me shall never thirst.

Ps 78:24: He rained down Manna for the people to eat He gave them grain from Heaven.

When the Manna fell in the wilderness, it was God's provision for the Day. They said we remember the fish we ate in Egypt which "cost nothing." Neither did the Manna, it was FREE, on how we compare the things of the world to God's way to our demise.

God knows that He is God. Now He wants us to know that!

Numbers 11:31-33: The Quail, A wind from the Lord sprang up, and it brought Quail, "The meat they wanted for they were not satisfied with the Manna",God provided the Quail from the sea and let them fall beside the camp, about two cubits above the ground. The people rose all that day and all night and all the next day, and gathered the Quail. While the meat was yet between their teeth, before it was consumed, the anger of the Lord was kindled against the people, and the Lord struck down the people with a very great plague, the people who had the craving were buried there. AMEN

TREE OF LIFE

Genesis 2:9: The tree of life was in the midst of the garden, and the tree of the knowledge of good and evil.

Gen 3:24: He drove out the man, and at the east of the garden of Eden, He placed the cherubim and a flaming sword that turned every way to guard the way to the tree of Life.

Gen 3:22: Then the Lord God said behold the man has become like one of us in knowing good and evil. Now, lest he reach out his hand and take also of the tree of Life and eat and "Live Forever." God sent him out from the garden of Eden, and he drove out the man.

Rev 2:7: He who has an ear, let him hear what the Spirit says to the Churches. To the one who conquers I will grant to eat of the tree of Life, which is in the paradise of God.

Rev 22:19: If anyone takes away from the words of the book of this prophecy, God will take away his share in the Tree of Life and in the Holy City which are described in this book.

In God's mercy and His Love for us, is why He did not allow Adam to take from the Tree of Life and live forever, forever in a Fallen Nature. Now in his sinful, fallen state, separated for God now. To take from the Tree of Life and Live forever in a Fallen state. Having cancer, a broken leg, eyes blinded, arthritis pain, discomfort, and on and on with our human afflictions, with no death, no relief. That would be an eternal Hell, while living forever. Understand how much God Does Love Us.

Rev 22: Blessed are those who wash their robes, so that they may have the Right to the Tree of Life, and may enter by the gates into the city.

When we got Saved, were Clean, our robes have been washed in the Blood of the Lamb. Now We Have Right to The TREE OF LIFE, and the Lord wants us to take as much as we can from the TREE OF LIFE. We're not of the Fallen Nature anymore, the Tree is accessible to those who have been redeemed, bought back from the fall Adam. "Jesus IS THAT TREE!" AMEN

"BACK TO EGYPT"

If You will remain in the land, then I will build you up and not pull you down, I will plant you and not pluck you up, but if you say we will not remain in this land disobeying the voice of the Lord your God and say, no we will go to the land of Egypt, or for us today back to what God delivered us from. If you set your face to enter Egypt and go there to live, then the sword that you fear shall overtake you and there you shall die. If you go back to Egypt, you will see this place no more for I have warned you. That you have gone astray at the cost of your life. For you have not obeyed the voice of the Lord your God in anything he sent me to tell you. You know for a certainly that you shall die in the place where you desire to go to live. God has called us with a holy calling, paid the price to redeem us, Ransom us back to Him by his death and His Blood. For us to remain to stay and to fight the good fight of faith to remain in this land that he has placed Us in, planted us and not to uproot us. And remain faithful then we will eat the fruit of the land. Going back, back to our old ways turning our backs on this new life and Desiring Egypt, or the way things were before we got saved. Say no to God in our hearts but trying to retain him in our mind. The only thing that keeps us from going insane, remembrance that one time in our life we did repent, believe for a while then fell away, but thinking that we're okay in God's eyes when really we're not.

"THE FALL"

The Pharisees problem was the sin of pride, self-righteousness why I've never been in prison, I've never done drugs. The word says that we all, all have sinned and come short all. Therefore, all need a savior. Why because of the Fall of our parents Adam and Eve, sinned and were thrown out of the Garden of Eden. When they were thrown out, they were cut off from their relationship with God who created them. We're their children and are cut off through the fall. What's so hard that we have no understanding that were spiritually lost, blind, dull of hearing God's voice. Like Adam when he ran and hid himself from God for the first time. Adam heard God call his name but did not want to respond, due to shame for the first time in his life, he hid from God and "tasted what Shame felt like." Before they sinned, they never saw themselves naked. After the fall, their sin, they saw their naked state and hid from one another, and from God, but there is no hiding from God who sees all and knows all. When God said where are you Adam, God knew where Adam was. My thought, God was giving Adam a chance to own up to his sin and come out from hiding and say Here I Am Lord for I have sinned Lord forgive me. But his self, is Flash, his mind, his will would not allow him, for it had control over him now. He was still Adam but walking and being controlled due to the fallen nature that now controls all of us. But through God's love for His creation, Adam and Eve created in the image of God. God became a man call Emmanuel God with us and bought us, brought us back to himself through his death on the cross while we all are in the Fallen nature from God. God paid the price to redeem us back to himself Through his blood, for the life of man is in the blood. Jesus' blood was pure he was never under the curse that fell upon Adam and Eve, pure sinless blood The Life of Christ that redeems all who believed. Abraham's son Isaac, the blood of the ram, the blood on the doorpost, the blood of all the sacrifices in the wilderness, to the blood of lambs without blemish that the high priests in the temple once a year would sacrifice for forgiveness of sin, to the blood of Christ the last of the blood offering once and for all. God came himself the creator of man being crucified by what he created. If that does not humble you take your pulse, for he gave it to you in giving us the Breath of Life. AMEN

DAVID AND GOLIATH

(The uncircumcised Philistine defies the living God)

Saul clothed David with Saul's armor.

He put his helmet on David's head and clothed David with his coat of mail.

Then David strapped his own sword over Saul's armor and tried in vain to go.

But then David said to Saul, "I can't go with these. I haven't tested them."

(So, have we tested our armor that we got on the day of our salvation?)

So, David took all the armor off, took his sling and chose five smooth stones from the nearby brook.

And with his sling in his hand, he approached the Philistine, who was over nine feet tall!

His bronze coat weighed 125 pounds; he had a bronze helmet, and he even wore bronze leg armor. He even had a bronze javelin.

The shaft of his spear was as heavy and thick as a weaver's beam, and it was tipped with an iron spearhead that weighed fifteen pounds!

And he had an armor bearer to carry his shield.

Us, in our battle, we can't fight our fight with someone else's armor, with someone else's faith, with someone's testimony, with someone's else's victory.

We have to fight with what we have, with our own faith for the battle, with our own faith for the victory, with our own faith which leaves us with a legacy for others to follow.

David took what he had, that which he had tested and had been proven over and over. That which he was comfortable with. That which he had used when he would go after a lion or a bear that had taken a lamb from his flock. Going after them, striking them and delivering the lamb out of the enemy's mouth. "And if he rose against me, I would catch him, then I'd strike him and kill him!"

David was comfortable using the five stones that he had found in the brook.

Five smooth stones: one stone, a teacher; one, a preacher; one, an evangelist; one, a prophet; and another, a pastor.

All five for the ministry of the gospel.

Five smooth stones, in each of these ministries lives where the word of God has been tested in each of their lives.

When the word is first taken in, it's not yet ready to be preached or taught. It's rough. It's not until it has been washed of the water of God's word, over and over and over.

In our spirit, in our mind, until the edges have been worked off.

When the word that was spoken to us becomes smoother and smoother and ready to be thrown from the sling of our tongue.

This smooth word that was thrown does not curve. It hits the mark that it was intended for.

"In the natural, you cannot curve a cue ball. There are no seams for the air to curve. This perfect smooth word will do its job." The word of God is thrown with our Tongue, which is our Sling now to deliver the Word.

1 Samuel 18:12: "Saul was afraid of David because the Lord was with David but had departed from him."

Amen.

"I CAN QUIT TOMORROW"

Tomorrow Has no power or strength to initiate change into our life. Today, right now is where the power is! Waiting one more day is a decision to stay on your path.

When we stay too long at one place we become stagnant.

We are God's clay. He is molding each and every one of us.

II Cor 4:18: Look Not to the things that are seen, but to the things that are unseen. When the Unseen is revealed our walk of Faith becomes deeper more clear, when the Unseen becoming visible, or having a deeper understanding. With good understanding our vision becomes clear, so we can see a far-off. So, when that which is a far-off and presents itself, we have a good understanding and are not shaken. but encouraged for we saw it coming, and standing firm, trusting God in all things, for he holds our future in His hand...Isa 8:17: "I will wait for the Lord." If we get ahead of the Lord, we're on our own, he's the lamp that lights the way before our feet. God Knows Best. Patience is a virtue, patience weights, that's why it's called patience taking what is precious from us, 'Our Time." We See things a far-off bye, and through the spirit. When the lamp that lights our feet before our past, that's what we see. A natural lamp only lights the way just before us, a natural lamp does not shine far off to show us the way.

The lamp is for each step that we take in Christ. The lamp of the spirit will show us things a far-off by Faith, and in God's timing.

"WHEN FAITH BECOMES SIGHT"

Though My eyes have never seen you, my eyes of faith have. I see you in your word your word is a reflection of you, Who You Are. There will come a day when I see you face to face. Jesus said if you have seen me you have seen the father. Blessed are those who have not seen and yet believe. Greater are we John the Baptist, we who have not seen yet believe, greater than Doubting Thomas. Faith has eyes that can see what are natural eyes cannot see. By faith our feet walk a path that are natural feet will never walk nor See. Where there's no stumbling, no falling, no cataracts, no glasses no red eyes, no need to close our eyes and rest when he is our rest. There is no night there, the eyes of the Lord see the present the past and the future who can claim that? Lord when my Faith becomes sight. AMEN.

We're to hold onto God's word! Then having done all to stand. Everything we need for Spiritual sight and living in Faith is in the word of God, as applied to our lives by the Holy Spirit...A living relationship with our savior, transforms our minds.

Prepare to meet your God. Repent. Do we realize the "natural man" continues to be hardened to the reality of the truth.

With Paul being imprisoned believers learned to deal more directly with God themselves.

Our partnership in the gospel, that I will not be at all ashamed. Only let your manner of life be worthy of the gospel of Christ. Every knee should bow all in heaven and on Earth and under the Earth. Work out your own salvation with fear and trembling, do all things without grumbling or disputing. For they all seek their own interest, not those of Christ. For his sake I have suffered the loss of all things and count them as rubbish in order that I may gain Christ. By prayer and supplication with Thanksgiving let your requests be made known to God. For I have learned in whatsoever situation I am to be content. He has delivered us from the Dominion of Darkness and Transferred us to his Kingdom of His Beloved Son. He is the image of the invisible God. For by Him all things were created, and He is before all things, He is the head of the body, He is the beginning. In Him all the fullness Of God dwells, through Him to reconcile to himself all things making peace through the blood of His cross. He has now reconciled in his body, by his death. Set your mind on things that are above. Put to death therefore what is Earthly in you, and have put on the new self, which is being renewed in knowledge and whatsoever you do in word or deed, do everything in the name of the Lord Jesus.

"ADAM CREATED THEN EVE"

Genesis 2:7: Then the Lord God formed the man of dust from the ground and breathed into his nostrils the Breath of Life, and the Man became a living creature. V16 And the Lord God commanded the MAN saying, "YOU may surely eat of every tree of the garden, but of the tree of the knowledge of Good and Evil You Shall Not Eat, for in the day that you eat you shall surely die. V 21,22 Now the Lord God caused a deep sleep to fall upon the man, and while he slept took one of his ribs and closed its place with flesh. And the rib that the Lord God had taken from the man he made into a woman and Brought Her to The Man.

Genesis 3:1: Now the serpent was more crafty than any other beast of the field that the Lord God had made. The Serpent said to the WOMEN, not Adam, but Eve. Did God actually say, "You shall not eat of the fruit of the tree that is in the midst of the garden, neither shall you touch it least you died." You will not surely die. For God knows that when you eat of it your eyes will be opened, and you will be like God, knowing Good and Evil." V6 She took of its fruit and ate, she also gave some to her husband who was with her and he ate. I believe that the serpent beguiled, tricked Eve, by saying Did God Say. God told Adam not to eat from the tree. Adam told Eve God said that were not to eat from the tree of the knowledge of Good and Evil. For Eve was not yet formed when God told Adam. Adam got it first hand from God, Eve got it Second hand from Adam. So, Satan took advantage of Eve, by saying "Did God Really Say. We can lean on our understanding and say, I don't know for sure if God said that. Adam told me God said that, so in a way Eve getting it second hand, and Satan took advantage of that when she leaned on her understanding. "Did God Say That? We go to church and here our pastor preach. We can say is he really hearing from God firsthand, or am I just getting something second hand. When does every word of God become true, real to us. Learn a lesson. AMEN

"BIBLE THE ROAD MAP TO HEAVEN"

The Bible is the road map to heaven!

Ps 23: He makes me lie down, He leads me, He restores me, He guides me, for His namesake. The Bible is the GPS, the directions to eternal life. You have run your race you have fought the good fight. Therefore, your Crown of Glory awaits you.

God is Not only our road map to heaven, but also our Judge. We're going to be judge by every word that's written, and the life we have lived. God is not going to judge anything that's outside of his Word. So, we have the answers to are test!

I Chronicles 16:37&40: So David left Asaph and his brethren before the Ark of the Covenant of the Lord to minister before the ark continually, as each day's work required. V40 Who offer burnt offerings to the Lord upon the altar morning an evening, and to do all that is written in the law. Jesus fulfilled the law by his offering of himself. He says today just as you are the work is finished, He came did his Father's will. Those that are of the truth will hear His voice.

At the point of my greatest need you were there!

Help my mind and my flesh Lord to comprehend you. AMEN

"THE PARABLE OF THE FIG TREE"

Luke 13:5,9: Jesus told this parable: A man had a fig tree planted in his vineyard, and He came seeking fruit on it and found none. He said to the vinedresser, look, for three years now I have come seeking fruit on this fig tree, and I find none. Cut it down, why should it use up the ground? And he answered him, Sir, let it alone this year also, until i dig around it and put on manure. Then if it should bear fruit next year, well and good, but if not You can cut it down, Isaiah 61:3: To grant to those who mourn in Zion, to give them a beautiful headdress instead of ashes, the Oil of gladness instead of mourning, the garment of praise instead of a faint spirit, that they may be called oaks of righteousness, "the planting of the Lord" that He may be glorified. The Lord planted us in His vineyard the day that we got Saved. How were to grow, mature, sprout leaves, then to bear fruit. The fruit is for the feeding of the nations. When the Lord had come down now this the third year and finding no fruit, He told the vinedresser to Cut It Down, why should it take up space in the ground. But the vine dresser said Lord leave it alone this year also and ill dung about it, and when you come back and there's no Fruit, then You can cut it down. The vinedresser is the Preacher, the fig tree is someone in his congregation. There just not doing well, falling away, no prayer life anymore, not reading the word very seldom attending Church. When the vinedresser said let it alone this year also and ill dung about it. What he was saying to the Lord was. I'll take the person under my wing and be watchful over then. I'll help with their reading the word, praying to gather, teaching, studying the word together, to help this person "this Tree" in their growth. But when You come back next year and find no Fruit, then You cut this tree down. That's not for me to do, Your will be done. AMEN

"HIDDEN THINGS THAT YOU HAVE NOT KNOWN"

Isaiah 48:6: You have heard, now see things, and will you not declare it? From this time forth I announce to you new things, hidden things that you have not known.

There is so much in God's word that has never been discovered yet. It's an unending book, unending word, and Unending revelation of Jesus Christ and his kingdom. New things are being discovered daily, now that we see things will we not declare it. We have been given this inside for a reason, for a purpose. To heal the brokenhearted, to set the captive free, deliver those that are bound, by the revelation of the unending word of Lights. AMEN

"THE STRAIGHT AND BROAD ROAD"

Matt 7:13: Straight and narrow, and Broad Road. Enter by the narrow gate for the gate is Wide and the way is easy that leads to destruction, and those who Enter buy it are many.

Ps 16:11: You make known to me the path of life, that means we have entered.

II Peter 2:15: Forsaking the right way they have gone astray, "To forsake something we must have known it to forsake it."

II Peter 2:21: For it would have been better for them never to have known the way of righteousness then after knowing it to Turn Back.

For it would have been better for them that they would have never known the straight and narrow. To know the straight and narrow mean that we have walked on that road. For He could have never said that it would have been better that we never knew this road. For the gate is wide and easy to Destruction so wide that we can't see either side, No Danger, No

Careing, No Concern, Everything Okay, relax be merry for tomorrow it gets even wider.

Matt 7:13: And those who Enter in are Many. "We Cannot enter the broad Road," we're born on the broad Road, due to the fall. Christ has made a way call the straight and narrow. We enter the straight and narrow through repenting of our sins, asking Christ into our hearts, He Places our feet on the straight and narrow. Now that were on that road we still have a choice, our free will. We can choose to enter that gate call the Broad Road to Destruction after salvation. By denouncing Jesus Christ, quitting, giving up, stop seeking and knocking and asking. We want it our way.

EPHESIANS 1:17

Give you the spirit of wisdom and of Revelation in the knowledge of Him. This is what the spirit Within Me has revealed through revelation of God's word. God's word speaks, opening up to a new understanding, a new opening up and bringing the word of life into this day and age. From 2000 years ago to now. His word that only grows with every generation, illuminating our way in this life here and now, where we are. To continue to be the word of life, opening up and being revealed to those who are hungry. The hungry I will not turn away empty. Seek and you will find, knock and the door shall be opened. For the Mysteries of God to be revealed, which springs life in abundance, overflowing. To feed and encourage the receiver, and those are the ones the receiver of riches, life in abundance will flow. AMEN

MARK 2:5 JESUS SAW THEIR FAITH

When Jesus saw their Faith, he said to the paralytic, Son your sins are forgiven. Our Faith is not transparent, its a substance to Jesus. He can see our Faith, knows how we operate in it or not. Nothing is kept from Him, that's why we're not to lean on our understanding. Our understanding is earth bound, so we are to walk by Faith and not by sight. Sight is the fallen nature. That's why Adam and Eve saw each other naked, for the first time. Before the fall they were both naked. Their eyes had not been open to the fall. But when sin entered in, they saw themselves naked for the first time. They separated themselves and went and hid from each other, and from God. No one can do that. We stand everyday naked before God, for He does see all. He wants us to come to Him just the way we are, without Him calling. He made His call to us by His Life and His Death. If that's not enough then we are what the scriptures says that we are. Poor, retched, deaf and blind and dumb. Jesus has made the way who will follow. The song writer said, "Though none go with me, yet I will follow." We've been given enough through the mercy of Jesus Christ to follow. The song "I can hear the Savior calling, come and follow Me." His call goes out to all humanity, that's who He died for, All. Rom 3:10, "As it is written, none is righteous no not one. In their path are ruin and misery." Rom 5:12, "Therefore, just as sin came into the world through one man and death through sin and so death spread to all men because all sinned." V19, "For as by the one man's disobedience, many were made sinners. So, by the one man's obedience the many will be made righteous. 6:22 "But now that you have been set free from sin and have become slaves of God, the fruit you get leads to, and its end, sanctification, eternal life." AMEN.

"Ps 116:15 Precious in the sight of the Lord"

Ps 116:15 Precious in the sight of the Lord is the "Death of His Saints."

Or I die to the lust of my Flesh, to say "Self", that's Precious to God. Not a natural Death. If it's a natural death, then we have lost our Voice

Ezekiel 18:32: For I have 'No Pleasure' in the death of "ANYONE," declares the Lord God, so turn and Live. Turn from your ways and live unto the Lord. For he has no pleasure that we Die and not receive Him. So, turn and live, or repent from your ways and live unto the Lord.

Ezkiel 33:11: I have" No Pleasure" in the Death of the Wicked. But that the wicked TURN from his way and LIVE. "Turn from your evil ways, Why Will You Die, O house of Israel." "The Death that God is pleased with is that We Die to SELF. That the Spirit may have its way in our lives. "And we can reach others

"WE ALL HAVE SOMETHING TO SAY, "IF" WERE SAVED."

You ARE the Light of the world, LET Your light Shine. Matt 5;14.

Psalm 89:15 Blessed are those who have Learned to Talk about Christ who Walk in the light of His Presence.

Romans 11:33: Oh, the depth of the richest of the wisdom and knowledge of God!

His pads are Beyond Finding Out. So, we will not find the path of God in Our Own Wisdom, in Our Own Strength. His riches, His wisdom, His knowledge, are Beyond finding out with our Natural Mind, and He has made it that way that all must believe by Faith, that leaves no one out, and without an excuse!

Jesus asked the man how did you get into the wedding without a garment, and he was SPEECHLESS! We who are saved are not speechless. We have a testimony that will be required of us, Start There and Learn to be a spokesman.

Fear is a crippler, Fear gripped Adam and he was speechless, He wasn't speechless before the Fall. Adam talked with God in the cool of the evening, in the Garden of Eden. We who Are Saved has been bought back, redeemed from the fall. Jesus says to "LET YOUR LIGHT SHINE." He will never force Us, when He said, "Father, It Is FINISHED, Now we're to Live and Move and Have Our Being In HIM. When We Move, He Moves. When God Moves first then we Move that's not Faith." We're" to make Our Calling and Election Sure, We Are To Do That. So, we All have something to DO! It's the" Doer" that's Blessed AMEN

"GOD CALLED MOSES"

Exodus 3: Moses was attending his flock in the west side of the wilderness and came to Horeb, The Mountain of God. The angel of the Lord appeared to him in a flaming fire out of the Mist of a bush, he looks, and behold, the bush was burning, yet it was not consumed. Moses said, "I will turn aside to see this Great Sight, the bush was not burned." When the Lord saw that he Turned Aside to see, God Called to Moses out of the burning bush, Moses, Moses! and he said, here I am. Then the Lord said, I have surely seen the Affliction of My People who are in Egypt and I've heard their cry because of their taskmasters, I know they're suffering and I have come down to deliver them out of the hand of the Egyptians, and to bring them up Out of that land to a good and broad land flowing with milk and honey, to the place of the Canaanites, the Hittimotes, the Amorites, the Perizzits, the Hivites, and the Jebusites. "I Will send YOU" to Pharaoh That You may bring my people, children of Israel, out of Egypt. But Moses said to God, who am I that I should go to Pharaoh and bring the children of Israel out of Egypt? Moses said. God said but "I Will be with You," this shall be a sign for you, that I have sent YOU. Then Moses said to God, if I come to the people of Israel and say to them, the God of your fathers has sent Me to you, and they asked me, what is his name? what shall I say to them? God said to Moses, I Am who I Am, and he said to the people of Israel, I Am has sent Me to you. I promise that I will bring you up out of the affliction of Egypt to the land of the Canaanites, the Hittites, the Amorites, the Jebusites, a land flowing with milk and honey, and they shall listen to YOUR VOICE, and when "you go," you shall not go empty. The Moses answered, but behold, they will not believe Me or listen to My Voice. The Lord said to Moses what is this in your hand? and he said a staff, and he said, throw it on the ground. So, Moses through it on the ground, and it became a serpent and Moses ran from it. But the Lord said to Moses, put out your hand and catch it by the tail, so he put out his hand and caught it, and it became a staff in his hand that they may believe that the Lord, the God of their fathers, God of Abraham, God of Isaac, and the God of Jacob, has appeared to YOU. Against the Lord said Moses, put your hand inside your cloak, and he put his hand inside his clothes, and when he took it out behold, this was leprous like snow. Then God said, put your hand back inside your cloak. So, Moses put his hand back inside his cloak, and when he took it out, behold it was restored like the rest of his flesh they will not believe you, God said, to listen to first sign, they may believe the ladder sign. But Moses said to the Lord, oh my Lord, I am not "eloquent," neither in the past or you have spoken to your servant, but I am slow of speech and of tongue. Then the Lord said to Moses, who has made man's mouth? Who has made mute, or deaf, or seeing, or blind? Is it not I the Lord? Now, therefore GO and I Will Be With YOUR MOUTH and teach you what you shall speak But Moses said, "Oh my Lord, please send someone else." Then the anger of the Lord was kindled against Moses and He said, "Is there not Aaron, your brother, the Levite?I know that he can speak well. Behold, he is coming out to meet you, and when he sees you, he will be glad in his heart. You shall speak to him and put the words in His Mouth, and I will be with Your Mouth and with His Mouth and will teach you both what to do. He shall speak For You to the people, and he shall be Your Mouth and you shall be as God to him."

Exodus 32: When the people saw that Moses delayed to come down from the mountain, the people gathered themselves together to Aaron and said to him, make us gods who shall go before us. As for this Moses, the man who brought us up out of the land of Egypt, we do not know what has become of him. So, Aaron said to them, the Ring of gold that are in their ears of your wives, your son's, and your daughters, bring them to me. So, all the people took off the rings of gold that were in their ears and brought them to Aaron. Aaron received the gold from their hand and fashioned with a grains took and made a Golden Calf. And they said, these are our gods, oh Israel, who brought you up out of the land of Egypt. The Lord God said to Moses. Go down for your people whom you brought up all the land of Egypt, have corrupted themselves. They have turned aside quickly out of the way They have made themselves a Golden Calf and have worshipped and sacrifice and said, these are our gods, oh Israel who brought you up out of the land of Egypt!

As if God speaking to Moses, I Am, who I Am, was not enough. The burning bush that was not consumed. Moses throwing down his staff, and it becoming a snake, then picking it up with his hand and it became his staff again. Restoring his leprous hand from leprous Back to flesh again.

I say this, to say that God called Moses, not Aaron. God Called Moses to go down into Egypt and speak. God showed Moses signs that he would be with him, to deliver the children of Israel, just GO. Moses in a way talked God into letting Aaron go with him to speak for him. Moses did have a problem, and God knew all about it, yet "Moses was called to go and to speak." Now when Moses came down from the mountain with the Ten Commandments, who talked the children of Israel to make a golden calf, Aaron. When God calls Us to do something, He will make a Way, He will provide we're just two Move. God calls us, to be the light of the world. God said to Moses" I will send you, I will speak through you, and I will be with you. God told Moses you shall not go empty and I'll be with you, I'll go with you, I'll be there for you." As God said to Moses, He might say the same thing to us. That who has made man's mouth, Made the mute, or deaf, or seeing, or blind? Is it not I, the Lord? We are the ones to move, and We wait on others, We miss out on what God wanted to do through us. AMEN

"AND GOD SHUT THEM IN"

Genesis 7:1 Then the Lord said to Noah, Go into the ark, you and all your household, for I have seen that you are righteous before me in this generation. For in seven days, I will send rain on the earth forty days and forty nights. Noah did all that the Lord had commanded him. Noah and his sons and his wife and his son's wives with him went into the ark to escape the waters of the flood. After seven days the waters of the flood came upon the earth. And rain fell upon the earth forty days and forty nights. Noah and his son's Shem and Ham and Japheth, and Noah's wife and the three wives of his sons' with them had entered the ark. And those that entered, male and female of all flesh, went in as God had commanded him." And the Lord Shut Him IN." Noah did not have the right to shut the door. God Shut the door, God shut them in, and the world out. I believe anyone could have helped Noah, but this was just too much to believe. That it was going to rain, and that they would need a boat, "Ark." One example of staying where God said to stay in.

Exodus 12:5: They were to take a lamb without blemish, a male, then the whole assembly of the congregation of Israel shall kill their lambs at twilight. Then they shall take some of the blood, and take hissop and dip it in the blood that is in the basin, and touch the lintel and the two doorposts with the blood that is in the basin. "None of you shall "go out of the door of his house until the morning." For the Lord will pass through to strike the Egyptians. When He sees the blood on the lintel and on the two doorposts, the Lord will pass over the door and will not allow the destroyer to enter your houses to strike you. Verse 22, "None of you shall go out of the door of his house until morning." As Noah, God shut them in.

Joshua 2: Joshua sent two men as spies to go view the land, especially Jericho. They came into the house of a prostitute whose name was Rahab and "lodged there". It was told to the king of Jericho, 'Behold, men of Israel have come here tonight to search out the land. Then the king of Jericho sent to Rahab, saying, bring out the men who have come to you, who entered your house, for they have come to search out all the land.' But Rahab had taken the two men and had "hidden them", upon her roof and hid them with the stalks of flax. Now then, please swear to me by the Lord that, as I have delt kindly with you, you also will deal kindly with my father's house, and give me a sure sign. That you will save alive my father and my mother, my brothers and sisters, and all who belong to them, and deliver our lives from death.

The men said to her, our life for yours even to death! If you do not tell this business of ours. When the Lord gives us the land we will deal kindly and faithfully with you.

Then she let them down by a rope through the window. The men told Rahab that when we come into the land, you shall tie this Scarlet Cord in the window through which you let us down. You're to gather into" your house" your father and your mother, your brothers, and all your father's household.

Then, "If anyone goes out of the door of your house into the street, his blood shall be on his own head", and we shall be guiltless. But if a hand is laid on anyone who is with you in the house, his blood shall be on our head. And Rehab said according to your word, so be it.

AS Noah, the Israel Lights, and Rahab, ALL SHUT IN BY GOD FOR HIS REASON. HIS PURPOSE. Do not come out. Now that were Saved, stay in Him.

Live and move and have our being in Him. He will make the way! AMEN

Rahab the harlot ended up in the blood line of Jesus. Salmon the father of Boaz by Rahab and on and on. Till Jacob the father of Joseph the husband of Mary, of whom Jesus was born. Rahab married into the royal priest hood. A Canaanite but by faith a Jewish believer now. The chief of sinners is just as welcome as the greatest Saint.

ISAAC AND ISHMAEL

Genesis 17:15,21: God said to Abraham, as for Sarai, your wife, you shall not call her name Sarai, but Sarah Shelby her name. I will bless her, and moreover," I will give you a son by her", I will bless her, and she shall become Nations, Kings of peoples shall come from her. Then Abraham fell on his face and laughed and said to himself, shall a child be born to a man who is 100 years old? Shall Sarah, who is ninety years old bear a child? And Abraham said God, oh that Ishmael might live before you! God said, "NO, but Sarah your wife shall bear you a son", and you shall call his name Isaac. I will establish my Covenant"

"with him," as an Everlasting Covenant his offspring after him. As for Ishmael, I have heard you, behold, I have blessed him and we'll make him fruitful and multiply him greatly. He shall father twelve princes, and I will make him into a great nation, but I will establish my Covenant" with Isaac", who Sarah shall bear to you at this time next year.

Genesis 21:2: Sarah conceived and bore Abraham a son in her old age at the time of which God had spoken to him. Abraham called the name of his son who was born to him whom Sarah bore him Isaac. V8 And the child grew and was weaned, and Abraham made a great feast on the day that Isaac was weaned, but Sarah called the son of Hagar the Egyptian, whom Add born to Abraham, laughing. So, she said to Abraham, "Cast out this slave woman with her son, or the son this slave woman shall not be heir best my son" Isaac."

I Chronicles 16:15,16: Remember his Covenant forever, the word that he commanded, for a thousand Generations, the Covenant that he made with Abraham, his sworn promise to "Isaac".

II Chronicles 30:6: Oh people of Israel, return to the Lord, the God of Abraham, Isaac, "not Ishmael"

Psalm 105:9: The Covenant that he made with Abraham, his sworn promise to Isaac

Matthew I: The genealogy of Jesus Christ, Ishmael is not mentioned.

Romans 9:7,9: Not all are children of Abraham because they are his offspring, but through Isaac your Offspring be named. this mean that it is not the children of the flesh who are the children of God, but the children of the "promise" are counted as offspring. For this is what the promised said, about this time next year you will return, and Sarah shall have a son.

Hebrews 11:17,18: By faith Abraham, when he was tested, offered up Isaac, and he who had received the promises was in the act of offering up his only son, of whom it was said, "Through Isaac your offspring be named."

Mark 12: 26: In the book of Moses, in the passage about the bush, now God said to him, saying, "I am the God of Abraham, and the God of Isaac, and the God of Jacob."

Galatians 4:22: For it is written that Abraham had two sons, one by a slave woman and one by a free woman. but the son of the slave was born according to the flesh, while the son of the free woman was born through promise. now this may be interpreted allegorically, these women are two Covenants. One is from Mount Sinai, being children from slavery she is Hagar. Now Hagar is Mount Sinai in Arabia, she corresponded to the present Jerusalem, for she is in slavery with her children, but the Jerusalem above is free, and she is our mother. For it is written, rejoice oh barren who does not bear, Break Forth and cry aloud, you who are not in labor. For the children of the desolate one will be more than those of the one who has a husband. now you, Brothers like Isaac are children of promise, but just as at that time he who was born according to the flesh persecuted him who was born according to the spirit, so also it is now, but what does the scripture say?" Cast out the slave woman and her son", for the son of the slave woman shall "not inherit" with the son of the free woman. So Brothers, we are not children the slave but of the free woman.

"HOW CAN A YOUNG MAN CLEANSE HIS WAYS"

Ps 119:9,10: How can a young man keep his ways pure?

By guarding it according to your word. With my whole heart, I seek You, let me not wander from your Commandments. I have stored up your word in my heart that I might not sin against you. We have to know the word, that the word will help us, guard our ways. We have to know the word before we can Wonder from it. We're to store up the word of Life in our hearts, to where the issues of life come from. If we do not take heed to the word where in an ocean treading water by ourselves, our own strength to keep us from drowning. We refuse the word of God, which is our life jacket, are lifesaver. We're content to work in our own strength to stay afloat. When all alone He's there waiting to hear you, cry to him for your help. He's the savior we're all the drowning party. AMEN

"It wasn't the apple on the tree, it was the pair on the ground."

"QUOTES"

It's not what we want out of life, it's what life Jesus wants out of us, the precious Being Christ in US.

How can you lose someone who's already lost.

You're the voice when I cannot speak. Jesus said, "Open your mouth and I will fill it.

When the amen's are void so am I.

We have an alarm to wait up the fleshly man, the truth wake up the spirit in a man."

The biggest sermon is your smile.

How can we say Amen, if it's not understood, "Amen means so be it."

LUST

Lust can defeat love, cripple it, even put us in a position where it feels better than love. But beware! Lust is a deceiver!

Proverbs 7:22, "And he goes after her like an ox goes to the slaughter, not knowing what's before him."

This is speaking about a naive Christian, any Christian, that lust can attach itself to. Not knowing the outcome, he follows her impulsively, like a deer bound in a trap.

And he went after her, like a bull with the butcher, being gently lead. Like an ox lead to the slaughter not knowing that death awaits him. Like a fool steps into a noose, he follows her like an impulse, not knowing that it will cost him his life.

Until a dart strikes through his "LIVER"! Our Liver is the purification system for our body which keeps our blood clean.

We have a spiritual liver that has now been pierced by Satan's arrow! When our spiritual liver is not functioning anymore, anything can enter in that will defile it. And losing all discernment, we go after her, void of any consequence.

"She" can give us all the things "we want," but she cannot make us content and give us a good countenance.

"OLIVE TREE, GRAPE VINE"

Psalm 52:8: I am like a green olive tree in the house of God.

Isaiah 5:7: For the vineyard of the Lord of host is the house of Israel, and the men of Judah are his pleasant planting.

Jeremiah 11:16: The Lord once called you a green olive tree, beautiful with good fruit. v 17 The Lord of host, who planted you.

Hosea 14:6: His beauty shall be like the Olive, and his fragrance like Lebanon.

The Olive press was in the garden of Gethsemane. Producing clean oil of beaten Olives for the light to make a lamp burn continually.

Isaiah 63:2: Jesus trampled out the Grapes of wrath of God's vengeance upon humanity by taking it upon Himself. Why is your apparel red, and your garments like his who treads in the winepress? I have trodden the winepress alone, and from the people, on one was with Me. v5 I looked, but there was no one to help, I was appalled, but there was no one to uphold, so my own arm brought me salvation. Only Jesus could have tread the Wine press.

Isaiah 61:1,3: The Spirit of the Lord God is upon Me, because the Lord has anointed Me to bring good news to the poor, He has sent Me to bind up the brokenhearted, to proclaim liberty to the captive, and the opening of the prison to those who are bound. To proclaim the year of the Lord's favor, and the day of vengeance of our God, to comfort all who mourn, to grant to those who mourn in Zion, to give them a beautiful headdress instead of ashes, the Oil of gladness instead of mourning, the garment of praise instead of a faint Spirit, that they may be called oaks of righteousness, the planting of the Lord, that He may be glorified. v 10 For he has clothed me with the garments of Salvation, He has covered me with the robe of righteousness, as a bridegroom decks himself. As a garden causes what is sown in it to sprout up, so the Lord God will cause righteousness and praise to sprout up before all the nations.

I say all of that to say this! For the Olive to be used for its purpose, it must be crushed.

For the Grape to be made into wine it also must be crushed. Are We as being likened unto the Olive, and the Grape. Are we giving ourself up to be crushed, to go through God's wine

press His Olive press and be used of God? The Oil and the Wine the presence of the Holy Spirit.

AMEN

JOHN 15:16

You did not choose Me, but I chose you and appointed you that you should go and bear Fruit and that your Fruit should remain, so that whatsoever you asked the Father in My Name He may give it to you.

Galatians 5:22,23 The fruit of the spirit is Love, Joy, Patience, Kindness, Goodness, Faithfulness, Gentleness and Self-Control.

Takes time to produce Fruit, Fruit has its seasons. Love is a good way to start, having Self Control, Patience, working in Kindness, Faithfulness Gentleness, Goodness, with joy. This Fruit is born through testing, our trials, our Temptations, our rising up and our falling down.

John 15, God chose Us and appointed Us, that we SHOULD go forth and bear Fruit.

Isaiah 60:21: The branch of my planting, the work of my hands, that I might be glorified.

II Samuel 7:10: I will also appoint a place for my people and will plant them, Isaiah 61:3 So they will be called the Trees of Righteousness, strong magnificent, distinguished for integrity, Justice, and right standing with God, the planting of the Lord. Love God, be faithful and the fruit will Grow AMEN

We all need the grace of God that Rahab experienced. The women at

the well, women caught in adultery. They knew that they needed Him.

"POOL OF BETHESDA"

John 5, Pool of Bethesda there lay multitude of invalids, blind, lame and paralyzed waiting for the move of the water. At certain seasons an Angel would stir the water, whoever stepped in first was healed. One man was there for thirty-eight years. Jesus said do you want to be healed. The man answered Him, sir I have no one to put me into the pool. God's waters are always moving, the fountain of life, rivers of living waters, streams in the desert.

Isaiah12:3: Draw waited from the wells of Salvation Isa 35:6: For waters break forth in the wilderness, and streams in the desert. Though we are all sick, lame, blind, and cannot move to get into the stirring of the water. We all have a Heart, emotion, it's from our Heart we move, from our Heart we take a step, that God will not deny. With our Heart we step into the pool of Bethesda. Our Heart helps us into the water, though we feel that we cannot move, Our Heart has a voice that God hears when we call out to Him.

louder than our body that cannot move. Isaiah 58:11: "After stepping in?" You shall be like a watered garden, like a spring of water, whose waters do not fail.

Ezekiel 36:25,27: I will sprinkle clean water on you, and you shall be clean from all your uncleanness, and from all your idols I will cleanse you. And I will give you a new heart, and a new Spirit I will put within you. And I will remove the heart of stone from your flesh and give you a heart of flesh. And I, will put my Spirit within you, and cause you to walk in my statutes.

Eph 5:26: That he might sanctify her the Church, having cleansed her by the washing of water with the Word. AMEN

"RETURN FAITHLESS ISRAEL"

Jeremiah 3:12, Return faithless Israel, "We are the Israel." Declares the Lord, I will not look on you in anger, for I am merciful, declares the lord. I will not be angry forever. V14 Return o faithless children declares the Lord, for I am your master, I will take you one from a city and two from a family and I will bring you to Zion "Your resting place." V15 I will give you shepherds after my own heart, who will feed you with Knowledge and Understanding. V17 They shall no more stubbornly follow their own evil heart. 4:1 If you return O Israel declares the Lord, to me you should return. If you remove your detestable things from my presence and do not waver. V3 Break up your fallow grown, V4 Circumcise yourself to the Lord, remove the foreskin of your Hearts. V19 I cannot keep silent, for I hear the sound of the trumpet. 7:23 Obey my voice and I will be your God, and you shall be my people. Walk in all the way that I command you that it may be well with you. 13:17 But if you will not listen, my soul will weep in secret for your pride. My eyes will weep bitterly and run down with tears. Because the Lord is our righteousness. 24:7 I will give them a heart to know that I am the Lord, and they shall be my people and I will be their God, for they shall return to Me with their whole heart. AMEN.

"LUKE 2:25,35" SIMEON

Now there was a man in Jerusalem, whose name was Simeon, and he was righteous and devout, waiting for the consolation of Israel, and the Holy Spirit was upon him. It had been revealed to him by the Holy Spirit that he would not see death before he had seen the Lord's Christ. And he came in the Spirit into the temple, and when the parents brought in the child Jesus, to do for him according to the custom of the Law, he took him up in his arms and blessed God and said, Lord now you are letting your servant depart in peace, according to your word. For my eyes have seen your Salvation that you have prepared in the presence of all people, a light for Revelation to the GENTILES, and for glory to your people Israel. And Simeon blessed them and said to Mary his mother, behold this child is appointed for the fall and rising of many in Israel, and for a Sign that is opposed, and a Sword Will Pierce Through Your Own SOUL. Simeon, righteous, devout, and the Holy Spirit was upon him. He came into the temple and the Spirit came upon him. Said a light for revelation to the GENTILES. Did the people miss the revelation of A Light for Revelation to the GENTILES, specking by the Holy Spirit. When Israel was thinking the Christ was there redeemed. That's why later, the Lord sent Paul to the GENTILES, for the hardness of their hearts. Thinking that Christ was theirs. I believe when Simeon told Mary that a Sword will pierce through your Own Soul also, meaning that the same conviction that pierced our Soul and we got Saved. That this same Sword would Pierce her Soul also. All need to come to Christ, one Door Open that all stand and knock for entrance, ALL. AMEN

"A COLT TIED, ON WHICH NO ONE EVER SAT"

Matt 11:1,2 Jesus sent two of his disciples, and said to them. Go into the village in front of you, and immediately as you enter you will find a Colt tied, on which "no one had ever sat," and bring it. V7 And they brought the colt to Jesus, and threw their cloak on it and He sat on it. And many spread their cloaks on the road, and others spread leaf branches that they had cut from the fields. "To me," the miracle is that Jesus sat, and road on this colt that had never been ridden before. The Colt was big enough, strong enough to carry a man, but did not buck, Jesus off, He Jesus was in control of this colt and rode into Jerusalem. "My thought," I could just see me riding a colt that had never been ridden before. I believe he would have thrown me off, and I would have no control of this animal. The Donkey reminded me of myself. How many times before I got saved, did i buck Jesus off and not wanting Him to control, or ride me. I was going to do it My Way, Disaster! AMEN

"AS POOR YET MAKING MANY RICH"

II Cor 6:10: As yet making many rich. 4:7 We Have this treasure within us.

James 2:5: Has Not God those who are poor in the eyes of the world, to be rich in faith, and to inherit the Kingdom, for those who love him.

Prov 10:22:The Blessings the Lord, it makes truly rich. We need to experience God's riches to appreciate them. Who said that we are rich, but do not spend it we are more than a fool? The man built his barns to store his riches, but never spending the ultimate Riches of God. His word to others that they may become rich. in faith, good works, rich in trusting when all else fails, rich in sitting at the table with God consuming the best meal ever made, which took His Life to make for us, that we might enjoy.

Ps 36:8: You Cause them to drink of the Stream of your pleasure. For in you is the Fountain of Life.

John 7:37: If any man is thirsty let him come to me and drink. V38 Then from his innermost being shall flow continuous springs and rivers of Living Water, "by the spirit. he spoke hear of the spirit", a stream that never stops flowing, no end to these riches that we give away by speaking the water of his word. The more we speak the more we have to give. There's no limit to his ability this Talent. The Lord says open your mouth wide and I will fill it. this takes faith, if we say we have faith it will be tested.

Prov 17:3: But The Lord tries the heart.

Ps 26:2: Examine me oh Lord and prove me.

Jeremiah 17:10 I the Lord, I try the heart, even to give to every man according to his heart, according to the fruit of his ways, his doings. We are the planting of the Lord, we're the tree he's planted. Now we're to have leaves that are for the healing of the nation, to bear fruit 12 months a year Rev 22:1-3.

Ps 20:2: Examine me oh Lord and prove me.

"BE STILL AND KNOW THAT I AM GOD"

Be still, how can I be still. We live in such a high pace, high speed, I want everything right now Society. Be still, why I am losing my precious time, I can't be just idle, there's too much that has to be done. Jesus said follow me, how do we follow someone we can't see. The disciples followed for 3 and 1/2 years, and then forsook Him. They saw Him, lived with Him, ate and drank with Him then forsook Him. Jesus said without Faith it's impossible. Are following Jesus now requires Faith. Faith and believing, Faith entrusting, Faith in obeying. He said He would send the comforter, who would teach, lead, guide, and direct us. By faith we are attached to Christ. The Pharisees Obeyed in their own strength, their own self effort. That's when Pride enters in, look what I have done, look how I obey. The scripture says, are striving is but losing, failing.

Romans 3: 27,28: What Becomes of our boasting? It is excluded. By what kind of law? A law of works No, by the law of Faith. We hold that one is justified by Faith apart from the works of the law. Be Still and Find God Working In Us. Be Still and Allow Him To Work, then you will See God.

I question the word of God. Seek and you'll find. Not someone else, me. What are You finding that You could write something about? If not for anybody but yourself. Growing producing fruit, preaching to yourself. putting the word of God on You the Tree in God's Vineyard, God's Garden. So, when he comes down that he might find fruit growing. He will inspect and it's for our good.

"BREAD FROM HEAVEN"

John 6, Our fathers ate the Manna in the wilderness, He gave them bread from Heaven to eat. My Father gives you the true bread from heaven. For the bread of God is He who came down from heaven and gave life to the world. I am the bread of life, whoever partakes of Me shall not hunger, and whosoever Believes In Me Shall Never thirst, as Jesus said to the woman at the well.

Luke 11:28 Blessed rather are those who hear the word of God and keeps it, keep it in our makeup, and our hearts.

Luke 6:45: For out of the abundance of the heart his mouth speaks what's in our hearts that we can talk about.

John 4:14: Whosoever drinks of this water that I will give him will never be thirsty again. The water that I will give him will become in him a spring of water Welling up to Eternal Life.

Song, Fill my cup Lord, I Lift It Up Lord, come and quench this thirsting of "my soul." Bread of Heaven feed me until I want no more, fill my cup. Fill it up and make me whole. AMEN

"And they sewed fig leaves together to hide their shame,"

Genesis 3:6,7

When the woman SAW that the TREE was good for food, and that it was a delight to the eyes, and that the TREE was to be desired to make one Wise, she took of its fruit and ate, and she also gave some to her husband who was with her, and he ate. Then the EYES of Both we're OPENED, and THEY KNEW that they were naked. And, "THEY sewed fig leaves together," and made themselves loincloth, to cover their nakedness.

Adam and Eve had one commandment from God.

Genesis 2:16,16 And the Lord God commanded the man saying, you may surely eat of every tree in the garden, but of the tree of the knowledge of good and evil you shall not eat, for in the day that you eat of it you shall surely die.

And we might think that we can keep the Ten Commandments, when Adam and Eve who were perfect could not keep one. That's why Jesus Christ had to come.

"The tree was desired to make one wise." They we're living with the one who has all wisdom, all knowledge, all understanding, they just needed to ask HIM. Colossians 2:2,3, "To reach all the riches a full assurance of understanding and the knowledge of God mystery, which is Christ, in whom are HID All the treasures of wisdom and knowledge. Jesus Christ is the tree of knowledge, and all wisdom, that we can partake of now."

Proverbs 3:7: Be not Wise in your Own eyes.

3:13: Blessed Is the one who finds wisdom, and the one who gets understanding. For The gain from Her is better than gain from Silver and Her profit better than gold. She is more precious than jewels, and nothing can compare to Her. Long life is in Her right hand, in Her left hand are riches and honor. Her ways of pleasantness, and all her paths are peace. She is a TREE OF LIFE to those who lay hold of Her. Do not lose sight of these, sound wisdom and discretion, and they will be life to your soul. "She being the Wisdom of God here."

Proverbs 4:7: The Beginning of wisdom is this, get wisdom, and whatever you get, get understanding It's ours for the asking. No longer fig leaves to cover our shame, and nakedness. We are clothed by God with the Garments of Salvation, through repentance. Adam and Eve died that day, it was the death of the Spirit. That's why Jesus said that we must be born again. Born of the spirit that died in the garden. The flesh lived on and was very much alive, but the spirit died that day. We must be born again from the fall of Adam and Eve. Jesus Christ came to restore that broken relationship. AMEN

"POOR IN SPIRIT"

Those who are poor spirit, kneading lifted up, minister to, having words of encouragement, strengthening words, words of life spoken unto them. That the week can become strong and can be used of God. When self is out of the way we can see that we need God and His help, His strength, His ability His power working in US and through our weakness we are made strong. For now, we can see that it's Christ working in US and not we ourselves. This is the victory that overcomes. We need to experience that in our walk, that Thrills us and we're looking for the next High and want to experience the move of the spirit. David was just a small boy the last of Seven Brothers who were bigger than David and stronger than David, but they weren't called, they were not anointed, and they were afraid of Goliath the giant before them. We all have Giants before us every day do we conquer or cower down. eventually our conquering should out number our failures, and that's what they are. If we fail the test God will have us take it again, until we pass and when we pass, what can stop us. Only ourselves let's get off of the milk and onto the meat of God's word, That will Keep Us, strengthen us to give us the ability to carry out God's word. AMEN

HOW ARE YOU WAITING

How are you Waiting? Not what are you waiting for, but how are you Waiting?

He has set us free. In being bound to the truth that set us free.

John 8:32: Being bound to Christ we walk in the newness of life. Bound to Christ that we no longer are slaves to sin. For the law had dominion over us, we were bound. Now we're bound to God's grace that sets us free. Now present your members as slaves to righteousness leading to our Freedom. The fruit that is produced leads to freedom and it's end eternal life.

Deuteronomy 15:12: If your brother a Hebrew man a Hebrew woman, is sold to you he shall serve you six years. In the seventh year you shall let him go, free from you. But if he says to you, "I will not go out from you," because he loves you and you're household he is well off with you. Then you shall take an awl, put it through his ear into the door and be your slave forever. A servant, slave, bound and loving the freedom being bound to his master. Now we are free when we're bound to Christ. This is beyond human reason or understanding. AMEN.

"CHANGE THAT "NAME"

Luke 1: 11,13: And there appeared to him and ANGEL of the Lord standing on the right side of the altar of incense. And Zachariah was troubled when he saw Him, fear came upon him. But the ANGEL said to him, "Do not be afraid," Zechariah for your prayers have been Heard, and your wife Elizabeth will bear you a son, and you shall call His NAME John.

V 59 And on the eighth day they came to circumcise the child. And they would have called him Zachariah after his father, but his mother answered, "No, he shall be called John." and they said to her, "None of your relatives it's called by that name," and they made signs to his father inquiring what he wanted him to be called. He asked for a Writing Tablet and wrote, "His name is John." And they all "Wondered."

Matthew 1:20, 21: An Angel of the Lord appeared to Joseph in a dream." Joseph, saying Son of David, do not fear to take Mary as your wife for that which is conceived in her is from the Holy Spirit. She will bear a

Son, and you shall CALL his name JESUS. V24 Joseph woke from sleep, he did as the ANGEL of the Lord commanded him, he took his wife, but knew her not "Until she had given birth to her first born Son. and he Called his name Jesus.

John 1:1: In the beginning was the WORD, and the WORD was with God, and the Word WAS God. V14 And the WORD became flesh and dwelt Among Us. "The WORD WAS GOD" When the WORD became Flesh and dwelled Among Us, the WORD took on the Name Jesus, Emmanuel, GOD WITH US.

In Luke, the people did not understand why his name was called John. That was not his father's name, and none of his relatives were called by that name.

In Matthew, the Angel said to Joseph that His Name shall be called Jesus.

Now today, we are still trying to do away with that NAME, which was given by the ANGEL, anything other than Jesus. We stifle it, quiet it, silence it, stomp it out, eradicated from our language and are thinking.

Like in Zacharias' day, the people Did Not Understand why he was called John? While we're still wrestling today with the name Jesus given by the ANGEL.

Matthew 28:18: Jesus said to them, all authority in Heaven and on Earth has been given to ME. "Were not to Lean on our own understanding." AMEN.

"COMPLAIN"

Complain is to slander His sovereignty, assault His lordship. We accuse God of being a bad father, when He's trying to correct us.

Complaining is giving expression to one's self-centered discontentment. It's our heart murmuring with vocal cords!

Grumbling and complaining comes from a root of bitterness that is so deep within our core that we are blinded when it comes out of our mouth. Discontentment and bitter attitude can become a sinful cancer, can't see it, can't feel it growing.

If we're Justified in our complaining, no matter how Justified I feel in my complaining, it leaves us worst then before. Deeper into depression, leading to anger bitterness, and discontent. When we complain, were saying that what the Lord has given us is not enough, when he knows best what is for us, not we ourselves. We're to stop complaining for the sake of our witness as a Christian. We say that God is good, but our dissatisfied grumbling is a contradiction to what we say we believe. Do we know that God knows all things work for our good and His glory?

Philippians 2:14: Do everything without complaining or arguing. We can become a pro at complaining and not see it ourselves, when others do. And that is what Christ looks like to them, why should they partake in something they already have?

"GOD'S SCALE"

Prov 11:1: False balance abomination to the Lord. God's scale there's no getting around it.

Luke 1: 51,53 He has shown with his arm, He has scattered the proud in the thoughts of their hearts. He has brought down the mighty from their throne and exalted those of humble estate, He has filled the hungry with good things, and the rich He has sent away empty.

The scale what's in the balance. He has scattered the proud in their thoughts of their heart, thoughts are weighty on God's scale. The rich He has sent away empty, not rich in wealth or money, but rich Within their own heart, They're rich in there wisdom, God Weigh haughtiness, someone who thinks he knows it all. He has filled the hungry with good things. Good things have a weight on God's scale. God weighs our hearts, not the one that pumps blood through our bodies. He weighs the heart of the matter. You might weigh 200lbs in the natural, but on God's scale we way just 16 ounces. Or we might way 98lbs in the natural, but on God scale we weigh 210lb, Faith has a weight.

The five wise virgins told the five foolish virgins, go to those who sell and by. Who is selling it, what are they selling, and what do they buy it with Face, is the economy of God. God weighs our Faith and He knows how much we have. If we want something on God's counter that cost $0.75, and we only have $0.12 of faith. God says come back another day when your face has grown, when we're rich in Faith, believing and in abiding, living out our faith. There is no limit how rich in God we can be, with no outward sign that we're rich. The Widow lady put in two mites she was very naturally poor, but Jesus said that she put in more than them all, she was rich in God, rich in Faith. God weighs the matter on His scales.

Isaiah 39: Prepare the way of the Lord, make straight in the desert a highway for God. Every Valley shall be lifted up, "Every humble lowly in heart will be lifted up for God to use." Every Mountain and Hill be made low, those who mighty think Highly will be made low to be used of God in his way. The uneven ground become level, and the rough places a plane. Behold His reward is with Him, and His recompense before Him, "To Render for compensation to his Saints." He weighed the mountains on His scales and the Hills in the balance. His understanding is unsearchable, He gives power to the faint, and to him who has no might he increases strength, until all is level now to be used. Those who wait for the Lord shall renew their strength, they shall mount up wings like eagles, they shall run and not be weary, they shall walk and not faint, just don't get ahead of the Lord. Then we will all function as one. For I Am With You, I will strengthen you, I will help you, I will uphold you.

Isaiah 41: 17,20: When the poor and needy seek water, and there is none, and there tongue is parched with thirst, I the Lord will answer them, I the God of Israel will not forsake them. I will open rivers on the baron Heights, and fountains in the midst of the valleys. I will make the wilderness a pool of water, and the dry land Springs of water. I will put in the wilderness the cedar, the acacia, the myrtle, and the olive. I will set in the desert the cypress, the plane and the pine together, that they may see and know, may consider and understand together, that the hand of the Lord has done this, the Holy One of Israel has created it.

To me the planting of all these trees, are different ethnic groups of those people. People from every tribe, Every Nation, getting saved all coming together in what was once a desert, now watered by God that we all may grow and come together as one. What God has put together, what God has cleansed, those who God has saved. AMEN

"COMING UP SHORT"

Scripture says Cease from your own labors. We spend our precious time laboring for that which Cannot Satisfy. At the end of our life coming up empty. Empty of peace and contentment we have labored for that which does not profit, empty and we knew that we were empty. For are striving, are working it out, our efforts fall short. Jesus said that without Me You Can Do Nothing. Yet our self will Rises up and says you Can. Finding out when it's too late that we Never Could. That's why Love Came to Us. Love is so powerful it even controlled God. He came to Earth because He Loved Us His creation. We have no understanding, for that which He created has put Him to Death. That's what Working in Our Own Strength Produces DEATH.

"WERE TO BEAR FRUIT"

Galatians 5:22

If we are saved, we are a tree, planted by the rivers of Living Water.

We are to bear fruit, for the fruit of the spirit IS love, joy, peace, patience, kindness, goodness, and faithfulness.

Gal 6:8: The one who sows to the spirit will from the spirit reap eternal life

Luke 13:6,8: This man had a fig tree planted in His Vineyard, and the Lord came down seeking Fruit on that Tree and found None! Who are we to say to the Lord, that he can't inspect US, He can't check out My Fruit. We are His Tree, planted in His garden, His Vineyard and He's coming down To inspect our Fruit, or to see what are We doing. It's best that He comes and checks on us now, before it's too late, when his checking will be death for Me

V9 The Gardener says, "If it should bear Fruit Well and Good. But if not YOU Can Cut It down." AMEN

"JESUS HAD BROTHERS"

Matt 1:25: Joseph knew her NOT, "until" she Mary had given birth to her first born son, and called his name Jesus.

John 7: 3: So, Jesus' Brothers said to Him, go to Judah that your" disciples," may see the Works you are doing. For Not even His brothers believe in Him. Jesus remained in Galilee but after his brothers had gone up to the feast, then Jesus went up. Jesus disciples were "all ready at the feast". These where Jesus Flesh and blood natural Brothers born through Mary.

AMEN

SAUL'S ARMOR, GOD'S ARMOR

Ephesians 6:13,18: Put on the whole armor of God, that you may be able to withstand in the evil day. The belt of Truth, breastplate of righteousness, shoes for readiness, the shield of faith, the helmet of salvation, sword of the spirit, which is the word of God, praying in the spirit. All the armor of God is on the front of his Saints, we should always be marching, moving forward, trusting the battle, in faith that the Lord goes before us into battle. That we have overcome and learning with each battle, each experience that our Shield of faith is working. That the sword of the spirit which is the word of God that we are learning to use. As the word of God sharpens our sword, the helmet of salvation always keeping in remembrance our testimony, and breastplate of righteousness that nothing formed against us shall prosper. AMEN

"NO GALLEY SHIP WITH OARS NOR MAJESTIC SHIP CAN PASS"

Isaiah 33:21: But there the Lord in Majestic Will Be for us a place of broad Rivers and Streams, where no Galley with oars can go, nor Majestic ship can pass!

Psalms 46:4: There is a river who's streams make glad the city of God, the Holy habitation of the Most High.

This is what I got from these passages. The Lord Majestic Will Be For Us a Place of Broad Rivers and Streams. The Lord has made, and the Lord has prepared a way for us, to travel His Rivers, His streams, by Faith and Faith Alone. No Galley Ship with oars, meaning we won't travel Gods Rivers in our own Strength, Our own understanding. The Galley ship is the ship with oars and usually two men to an oar to propel the Ship, to make the Ship move with Human Strength. God says you will not travel My River that way, by your own Strength. The Majestic ship is a ship with sails that the wind Moves Along, Not needing Man Power to move. The Majestic ship is one who is puffed up, proud of one's accomplishments, their own Wisdom, look at Me, neither ship will Sail on God's Rivers or Streams. There is a river whose streams make glad the city of God. AMEN

"THEY COULD NOT SEE THEIR PROBLEM"

Numbers 21:5: They had to look up to the serpent, but didn't see their Problem when speaking against God and Moses. Why did you bring us out of Egypt to die? For there is no bread, neither any water and we loath this manna, That is what they said, but could not see their own problem. God sent serpents among the people, and bit the people and many died. Moses made a serpent of bronze and put it on a pole. If a serpent had bit any man when he looked to the serpent of bronze he lived. We look up to God by looking down, Down On Our Knees with head bowed, then we are looking up. A broken and a contrite heart God will not despise. When we are humbling ourselves bow to submission we're looking up, that's God's way.

Like the Widow lady, putting in two mites in the offering. Jesus watching saw that she put in more than they all. For she put in from her want, or to say her lack, she put in her all. Trusting that God would provide for her. That is like going out on a limb Turning around and sawing the limb off behind you, knowing that He will catch us or just say He is our Provision. They had to look and see the bronze serpent on the pole, but they could not see their problem that took them there.

"WATER AND SALT"

Mark 9:41: Whosoever gives you a cup of water to drink because you belong to Christ will by no means lose his reward. Here we have someone giving a drink of water to another person who's saved. The water is the word of God spoken to this person. An unsaved person would not know or understand the water the word being spoken. A saved person giving another saved person a refreshing life-giving water from the word of life. Our Spirit drinks in this Living Waters or this Living Word. That refreshes One Soul and the one who's speaking the word is refreshed also. Those who hunger and thirst after righteousness will be filled. The spirit in one can ENCOURAGE the other.

Mark 9:50: But if we as salt has lost its Saltiness how will we make it salty again? have salt in yourself, without salt in our lives how can we salt or encourage others. Salt changes the taste of everything it comes in contact with!

Without salt in this person's life, v 41 this person would have not received his cup of water. Am I, are you, encouraging others with the salt that's within us, or have we lost our saltiness?

Matt 5:13: You are the salt of the earth, but if salt has lost its taste, its strength, its quality, how can its saltiness be restored? It is not good for anything, any longer but to be thrown out and trotted underfoot by men. That's What God Says. Are we still hiding like Adam hid himself when he heard God walking in the garden? Do we hear God walking around in our heart? Do we shut out his voice wishing that He would not call are name, are we still in hiding ashamed of our nakedness that He knows all about. I believe God called out to Adam in hoping, Desiring that Adam would have stepped out of his shame of his hiding? For the first time in his life, Adam had never hidden before. The world is still in hiding from God. God calling where are you Adam, meaning where is my Creation. I still long and desire for you, step out and come home. AMEN

"PSALM 23:5"

You prepare a table before me in the presence of my enemies.

To me the table that's prepared before me has the Word of God on it, the Bread of Life. I'm to devour that word which strengthens me, which gives me the right word to say in due season, to draw, to speak to my enemies in love, which conquerors those who have that ear to hear. AMEN

"MOUTH SPEAKS"

II Cor 4:4,6: The god of this age has blinded the minds of unbeliever, so that they cannot see the Light of the Gospel "HE" made his light shine in our Hearts to give Light of the knowledge of the Glory of God.

A good person brings Good out of the Treasure of Good things that are in his Heart.

A Bad person brings Bad out of his treasure of Bad things. For the Mouth Speaks What The Heart Is Full Of.

Our Heart has a Mouth, our Heart has ears, our Heart has feelings, emotions. From our Heart our lives are to be directed, a compass to guide us through our lives while here on earth.

Isaiah 55:8: For my thoughts are not your thoughts, neither are your ways my ways.

Romans 8:7: To set the mind on the flesh is death, but to set the mind on the Spirit is Life and Peace.

II Cor 4:4,6: The god of this age has blinded the Minds of unbeliever, so they Cannot See the Light of the Gospel. "HE" made His Light of the knowledge of the Glory of God

We set our minds from our Hearts where the Spirit of the person lives.

In our Head we have eyes, but we do not see, we have ears, but we do not hear, we have a tongue but it does not speak of the things of God. This is due from the fall. The scripture says that were deaf, dumb, and blind. Christ came to Save, to bring back to Life our fallen Spirit, the Spirit revived or renewed brought back into right standings which only He could do. Now that our Spirit has been renewed, brought into right standing, due to God's Love for us. We now can hear with our heart's ear, see with our Heart's eyes, speak from a new Heart. For out of the Treasure of this new Heart now flows the issues of true Life. We're not all His, God knows those that are His, or those that are in Him. Those who have stood at His door and knocked, and He opened unto them. Those are the ones that are His. Are you standing without today? AMEN

JOY IN SORROW

Psalm 126:5: Those who sow in Tears will Reap with Songs of Joy.

A slow song, seemingly sad song can be very Joyful in Heart. First, understanding what's being Sung. Revelation of a Sad Song, yet Bringing Great Joy, and Release to the Heart. For we Listen with Our Heart, Receive in our Heart the Joy it was meant to Bring. Though someone else's sorrow, Joy has sprung forth through Song.

"WERE NOT TO WALK IN THE FUTILITY OF OUR MINDS"

Ephesians 4:17

WE must not Walk As the Gentiles do, in the futility of their minds. They are darkened in their understanding, alienated from the LIFE of GOD, because of the ignorance that is In Them, due to their Hardness of Heart. Assuming that you have heard about Him, and we're taught in Him as the Truth is in Jesus. Put off your old self, which belongs to your former manner of life and Is Corrupt through Deceitful Desires, and Be Renewed in the Spirit of your minds, and Put on the New Self, created after the likeness of God and True Righteousness and Holiness. We can be Deceived and not knowing that we have been Deceived. Until we find out the Truth of the Matter that we Are Of The Fallen Nature.

Jeremiah 29:13: You Will seek Me and "Find Me," when you search for Me with All Your Heart. That's called coming to the end of ourselves, there we find Christ! If we never come to the end of ourselves, where left with self. We're going to do it our way, our strength, that we really are "Independent from Christ" that's being Deceived. AMEN

"COLOSSIANS 1:29"

For this purpose, I also labor, striving according to "His Power," which works Mightily in Me. His power working in US, something we have to find out, discover for ourselves. That's where Faith comes in. That Christ power is working in US. It's our job to test that power, to try that power, to prove to ourselves that it's real! God already knows it's Real, Do We. Let that which is born of God arise IN US! AMEN

"MY WAY"

This life that "I Thought" I could not do. This life that "I Thought" I could not walk. This Life that "I thought" is not for me. I've found that I can do. I can walk, I have found that it is for me! Through believing, through holding onto, trusting no matter what.

There is another way it's called "no way," and it has a lot of names. "The street of no end," "the street of no hope," "the street of no joy," "the street of no peace," "the street of no light," "the street of hopelessness," "the street of doom."

All of them lead to "the street of eternal death," which is an eternal road which has no end, and the Name of that street is called "My Way!"

Amen.

OUR FAITH BEING MORE PRESSUES THEN GOLD

I Peter 1:7: That the testing, trying, genuineness Of your FAITH being more Precious than GOLD!

Gold in the Bible is mentioned 417 times, silver 320.

Proverbs 3: 13,14: Blessed is the one who finds Wisdom, and the one who gets Understanding, for the Gain from Wisdom, and Understanding, it's Better than gain from Silver and her Profit better than Gold.

Psalm 119:127: Therefore, I love your Commandments above Gold, above Fine Gold. "By Faith we Believe, and Follow His commandments. In following his Commandments by Faith the True Riches of God are found above Gold.

Job 23:10: He knows the way that I take, when he has Tried Me, I shall come out as Gold. "Our Faith it's going to be Tested and Tried, to show, to prove what we are made of."

Proverbs 17:3: The Crucible is for silver, and the furnace is for Gold, and the Lord Test Our Hearts, "to see what we are made of" When the Lord test our Hearts, he's testing our Spirit to see what we are made of. Will we pass God's test and be more precious than Silver and Gold which will Perish, Our Spirit Is Eternal.

Psalm 19:7&10: The law of the Lord is Perfect, Reviving the Soul, the testimony of the Lord is sure, making Wise the Simple, more to be desired are they than Gold, even much fine Gold.

Acts 3:6: Peter said, I have no Silver and Gold, but what "I DO HAVE!" I GIVE TO YOU, Rise Up And Walk. Peter imparted Faith, Hope, and the man took a hold of That and Stood Up. Faith outweighs, out trumps, Gold and Silver." The man could have thought within himself, I'm not getting Gold, and I'm not getting Silver, but such as Peter has, I'm getting! And he Took Hold Of That and Stood Up.

Revelation 21:5: I am making All Things New.

V21 The street of the City was Pure Gold, LIKE TRANSPARENT GLASS.

We walk by Faith, our Faith is Transparent, God sees All, and our Faith is more Precious than Gold, Keep Walking were not to give Up. AMEN

II Cor 1:7: As you share in your suffering you will also share in your comfort.

Searching the word has become like digging for gold. The more I search, dig and discover I want to dig deeper for I'm finding out, there are true riches to be found in his word, which is understanding. If we seek, He said we would find, if we knock the door will be open. Now get ready for the responsibility of your seeking and asking and knocking. this which was found by you to share with others. But don't look at their faces, look at their spirit, their hearts, the real person that secretly cries out for help. In spite of what their mind is saying to them, I've been there. As in Adam, we run from truth, run from what is right for truth exposes the real self. Our whole life and all we have ever known is self and that's due to the fall. Nothing that we have done, we inherited It! One fall of Adam sin Came Upon all, all are broken. The righteousness of Christ wipes the Slate of our life clean. As if we have never sinned, something we have to experience while in this life. One fell, one Resurrected, faith is in the connecting Factor. Naaman had to dip seven times in the Jordan to be cleansed of his leprosy, a step of faith is all it takes, for cleansing, without faith it is impossible. AMEN

I Cor 12:18: But as it is. God arranged the members in the body, each one of them as He chose. V 23 and on those parts of the body that We Think less honorable He bestows the Greater Honor. V 24 God has so composed the body, giving Greater Honor to the part that Lack, having the same care for one another.

SALT

A master knows how to use Salt. he prepares a very expensive meal, and can ruin it with two little or too much Salt. We must watch our words, or to say the Salt of our words wisely. Too much Salt from the word of God and we can make God very distasteful to an unsaved person. Two little and God is barely noticed, or no Salt Due to fear, I'm not learned, I can't Witness, and on and on. We have our testimony how God made mention of us, and saved us call us, we carry the words of life and where to use it. by the word of God and our testimony, by the Blood of the Lamb, and the word of Our Testimony we overcome. How can anyone else get saved if we're ashamed of Our Testimony. Jesus said that if you are ashamed of Me, I'll be ashamed of you. God did his part and said father it is finished, it's done, it's accomplished.

Now what will my creation say and act like call on Me, or will they cry out and ask for the mountains to fall on them to hide them from the face of the Lamb.

PSALM 119:162

I rejoice at your word, like one who finds great spoil or treasure. Are we finding treasure in and from God's word? Seek, knock, and you will find.

Are we speaking, have we knocked and keep knocking, are we asking, and keep asking? Like the woman in the Bible going before the unjust judge. The judge who feared not man or God. But because of her continuing coming to the king, he gave what she wanted.

"DID GOD REALLY SAY?"

Genesis 3:1: Now the serpent was more subtle than any other Beast of the field that the Lord God had made. He said to the woman "Did God Really Say, 'You shall not Eat of the Tree that is in the midst of the garden.'" For God knows that when you eat of it your eyes will be opened. God said not to eat but they did and the Fall Entered In. Now, today our minds tell us not to read the word, not to believe the word, not trusting what the word can do in US. Our minds would say that's not real. Stay away from the word, man wrote it, can't be true.

Psalm 34:8: God says Taste and see that God is good, blessed is the one who takes refuge in Him! By faith, in believing that every word of God is true, then our Eyes will be Open, which Satan does not want. He wants us to remain Blind, Deaf to the word of God, the Word that brings forth

Life not Death. If we're not Saved, we are Dead while we live. the Word brings forth Life from that death. AMEN

HOSEA 6

Come, Let Us return to the Lord, for He has Torn Us, that He may Heal Us, He has Struck Us down, and He will build Us up. God has Struck Us and Torn Us that we would remember and not forget what We have done, and what We have been delivered from. A good reminder of where we were, and where we are now after God builds Us Up. V5 I have slain them by the words of my mouth. His Word is like a two-edged sword on the way in cutting and removing what's need's taken out. With healing and deliverance when withdrawn! 7:14: Yet some do not cry to Me from their Heart.

Jesus, if I stay here, I am only here. If I go away, I'm everywhere!

Passion for God keeps us fresh and equipped to recognize the hand of God.

When Passion dies, the Lamb of perception is eventually removed

The willingness to Bear reproach from our brothers and sisters is part of the cost we pay for the move of the spirit.

Quenching the spirit, it's probably responsible for the end of most revivals.

Watch That our desire to go to heaven is not stronger than seeking first the kingdom of God and his righteousness.

A Man in one of Jesus parable was cast into outer Darkness for he buried his "Money, Talent," and not obtaining and increase for his master

The Priest never sat down while doing the sacrifices in the holy of holyes, his work was never done, and if the Bells on the Hem of His Garment would stop ringing, they would drag him out with a rope that was tied on his foot for he was dead. Our work is not done Until we go to our Grave.

John 14:6: Jesus said I am the Way, and the Truth, and the Life.

Jesus is the Way out of the fall of Man, he is the Truth in this life while we live, and he is the Life in the Everlasting.

"POUR OUT YOUR HEART"

Pour out your heart, then where empty to be filled. We cannot fill ourselves so stop trying. For our trying are striving is but failure. He came to do what is impossible for us to do, and it took his life to accomplish that. Now He asked us to lay down our lives one day at a time, until we go and meet him. We die to self that we might truly live. His death brought life to us. When we die, true life comes into us. We're only on this Earth for a very short time compared to Eternity. Each and every one of us have an Eternal Spirit. given to us by God where will we spend it. AMEN.

"WINEPRESS"

The Wine press today is will we produce good grapes as his Noble Vine that He has Planted. When calling us by the spirit into repenting of our sins and asking him into our hearts, unto salvation. Now that we're growing in wisdom, growing in knowledge, growing in patience, growing in love, and coming to an understanding of His words of life. Are we ready to go into God's winepress to be crushed and Used to become the wine of the New Testament, to be poured out to others who are thirsty. We're to be tested, tried, and proven worthy. Come and taste and see that God is good. The only Christ some people we'll see is Christ in US, how are do we represent him. AMEN.

"THEY WHO WAIT FOR THE LORD"

Isa 40:31: For those who wait upon the Lord. Waiting on the Lord takes strength, stamina, endurance, long suffering, patience. It can be work, because we are impatient. They will renew their strengths. To be renewed we must have been doing something. If we're not doing much or anything, why should we be renewed? We're not using what we have been given. they shall Mount up with wings like eagles. Let's hope that this is not our first time of mounting up are wings like eagles and soaring in God's presence. Run and not be weary? When's the last time we have run to and for God. Running builds up stamina, like the Boston marathon runner is conditioned. Where to walk and not faint, when we are rejected for what we stand for and believe in, trusting adhering to hope in this Life, and the one to come!

"KING AHASUERUS AND QUEEN ESTHER AND US!

"From the book of Esther." Start in chapter 3:13. Letters Were sent by Courier to all the king's Providence with instructions to destroy, to kill, and to annihilate all Jews, young and old, women and children in one day. The letter of the law says, the soul that sin shall Surely die. We are of the Fallen nature, so the human race is on that list, that letter. 4:2 Mordecai went up to the entrance of the Kings gate, for no one was allowed to enter the Kings gate clothed in sackcloth. Today, Without repentance, there is no entrance, a broken and a contrite heart God will not despise, Come As You Are. 4:11 All the king's servants and the people of the Kings Providence knew that if any man or woman goes to the king inside the inner Court without being called, there is but one law, to be put to death. Except the one to whom the king holds out the golden scepter so that he may live. No one can come unless the spirit draws. now that Jesus has risen from the dead, all can come now. But repentance is required to enter, a broken and a contrite heart the king will not despise, that's King Jesus. 4:14 Now, in your life is this now your appointed time to come before the king, just as you are allowing entrance, and allowing us to touch his golden scepter as he holds it out that we have been accepted in the beloved Jesus. Enter now. Are we silent and not going to the king that would be what are flesh would want? Queen Esther sent garments to clothe Mordecai so that he might take off his sackcloth. The spirit of God wants to give us a new white robe, now that we're saved, the Garment of salvation.

Matt 22:11: The king came in to look at the guest, he saw there a man who had not the wedding garment, and said to him, friends how did you get in here without a wedding garment, and he was "Speechless." For many are called but few are chosen. we're not to be found Speechless on that day when it's required of us. There's no time to get ready then. We're either ready now or we're not, choose you this day who you will serve, the flesh unto death or the spirit until life. The way has been made for us.

For those who have ears let them hear what the spirit says to the church. "We the people"

I Tim 6:12 You have fought the good fight of Faith, now take hold of eternal life to which you were called. making a good confession in the presence of many witnesses. AMEN

EZEKIEL 3:10

Son of man, all my words that I shall speak to you receive in your heart, and hear with your ears. Speak to the people and say, "Thus says the Lord God, whether they hear or refuse to hear, for they have a stubborn heart. But he who will hear, Let Him hear, and who will refuse to hear, Let Him refuse. For they are not willing to listen to me. But when I speak with you, I will open your mouth, and you shall say to them. I warned you Wicked of your wickedness to turn from your Wicked Ways. And he does not turn from his wickedness he shall die for his iniquity, but you will have delivered your soul. But if you give the wicked no warning, nor speak to Warren the wicked from their ways, in order to save his life, that Wicked person shall die for his iniquities, but his blood I will require at your hand. Be ready instant in season and out of season, ready to give and answer to those who ask of the hope that lies within you. For I will put an end to the pride of the strong according to their ways, I will judge them, for they say the Lord does not see. Therefore, my eyes will not spare, nor will I have pity, and though they cry In my ears with a loud voice, I will not hear them. But if they remove their detestable things they're Abominations, then I will give you one heart, a new spirit I will put within you. I will remove Your Heart of Stone, and give you a new heart that you may walk in my statutes, my ways and Obey them. I will be your God. AMEN

"MATTHEW 6:33"

Seek first the Kingdom of God and his righteousness.

Christ is real, like the air we breathe. Can't see it, but it's there, giving us life! Jesus is there to give life back to the falling man. The spirit does not need oxygen to sustain life, but our flesh does. The spirit needs its closeness to Jesus, the Giver of eternal life where no oxygen exists. That's how much we need him! One day our oxygen will cease, come to an end. Just try to breathe then when life breathing oxygen no longer exists. Oxygen is for the fleshly man. The spirit given is for the new man. One surrendered to his maker where breath will be needed no more to sustain life. We will be in the presence of God. A place where oxygen is not needed to sustain life! We have spiritual lungs, it's our Face. When now we take in the Living Word, the bread of life, taking our drink from water of his word streams of life, waters that never cease.

John 4:32: Jesus said I have food to eat that you do not know about.

I Corinthians 10:4: All drank the spiritual drink. For they drank from the spiritual Rock that followed them, and The Rock was Christ.

John 6:35: I Am the Bread of Life. Whosoever comes to me shall not hunger, and whoever believes in me shall never thirst.

John 6:27: Do not work for the food that Parishes, but for the food that endures eternal life, which the son of man will give to you.

The word of God is alive and active to all who Believe. AMEN

"II CORINTHIANS 4:18"

Look Not to the Things that are Seen, but to the Things that are Unseen, for the Things that are Unseen Are Eternal.

Our natural physical eyes are for this life in the flesh. Scripture says that we are deaf dumb and blind, born that way from our mother's womb. That's why Jesus said you must be Born Again, behold all things will become new.

I see more with my eyes closed then I do with my eyes opened. We look not to the things that "Are "Seen" but to the things that are "Unseen," in the Spiritual Realm, does that help. He took out the Heart of Stone and has given us a Heart of Flesh, that's our New Eyes that can see a far-off, No glasses needed to see God's path, God's plan, God's will for our lives. Our Faith will become our sight. Then we will discover that we have New Ears also. AMEN

"I WILL STRENGTHEN YOU"

Isaiah 41:10: "I will strengthen you." One week quoting that scripture, and I see no change? After one week of working out in the gym are we going to see a change? So we Quit, we give Up, it's just too much work for what I put into it, and what I get out of it His word is our weights. His word is our treadmill, our elliptical, His word is are dumbbells, for His dumbbells "us. We're to exercise are Faith. Faith has no physical weight, but it's heavy and carry's weight. Weight to Concur to achieve the impossible. to be able to climb that mountain, to cross your desert, to sour and fly on high where the Flesh cannot take us. To be able to see a far-off, to run and not be weary, to walk by Face and not faint, to trust, to adhere to that which we cannot, until our face becomes sight. Then the Goliath's in our life Lays at our feet unable to move anymore. His head comes off with the sword of the spirit that has been worked in and through God spiritual gym ! Don't give up. Don't quit. There's no retirement from this service

Don't let our hearts be like the bags with holes in them. That what was just put in them has run out.

Haggai 1:6,14: You have sown much, and harvest little. You eat, but you never have enough, you drink but you never have your fill. You clothe yourselves, but no one is warm. And he who earns wages does so to put them into a "bag with hole" says the Lord of hosts, consider your ways. Go up to the Hills and bring wood and build the house that I may take pleasure in it and that I may be Glorified, says the Lord. You look for much, and behold, it came to little. When you brought it home, I blew it away. "Why? declares the Lord of hosts. Because now my house that lies in Ruins, while each of you busies himself with his own house. Therefore the heavens above you have withheld their due, and the Earth has withheld it produce. I have called for a drought on the land and the Hills, on the grain, the new wine, the oil. On what the ground brings forth, and on your labor. Then the people obeyed the voice of the Lord their God, and the words of Haggai the Prophet as the Lord their God had said to him. I am with you declares the Lord. and the Lord stirred up the spirit of Zerubbabel and all the remnant of the people, and they came and worked on the house of the Lord of hosts their God. "They came and worked." AMEN

"GOD NEVER CHANGES"

Hebrews 13:8: Jesus Christ is the same yesterday and today and forever.

Malachi 3;6: For I the Lord do not change,

John 1:1: In the beginning was the word, and the Word was with God, and the word was God. "God does not change and His word Remains the Same."

"He who never changes, nor will ever change, wants us to CHANGE."

He knows the future and what is ahead of us. Love wants us to CHANGE.

A willing heart CHANGE. To escape what is to come. He paid the price for our Escape, from Death to Life. He said I have come to set you Free!

"WORSHIP"

Worship is a weapon, surrender and give worship you're all. Allow yourself to enter in through surrendering, letting it go, giving up so God can come in, for you have made room for Him. You will want to do it again and again and again. God can take us away and we never leave the room, let him, allow him to move and have his way and be quiet in the Inner Man. Still yourself of the cares of this life. That we can have a taste of what it's going to be like. Jesus did say taste and see that I am good. It can be said experience me while you're in this life. That when you truly get home you will have already had a taste of this life, which is to come. Experience God now and you will not be the same. He said to lay your burdens down. That's anything that distracts us from entering into his rest. We need to experience Him while we are in this life. a glimpse of Glory, a touch of Heaven that causes us to yield, give up and let God move in our worship. Letting go of what would hold us back from entering in. Give Him fifteen minutes of your time, for His, which is eternal. God says come Just As You Are and experienced me! AMEN.

What we win people to, is what we win people with.

Don't let your Lives cloud, hinder what your lips want to say.

"SIN HAS COME BETWEEN US"

Have we found out that our sin has come between us and Christ. Our sin is the Veil and Christ did away with through his death. In the Old Testament, up to the death of Jesus when the veil in the temple was torn, from top to bottom that all can enter in now. We must deal with our sin that separates us from Christ. Through repentance and asking for forgiveness, calling on the name of Jesus, our Darkness now becomes light. Behold All Things become new, the old is passed away. Our dormant or dead spirit brought to life true repentance? Just through repenting having a broken and contrite heart which Jesus sees. The spirit has broken us. Broken to heal, broken to make right, broken that we now live. From Death To Life, blind but now we see. See what we have been missing. When he says behold All Things become new. From the old nature we cannot see what Christ has for us. Until our eyes are open in the newness of life. From the old man, if we could see what Christ has for us, we may never come. We're trying to see the new through the old man's eyes. Even if we could see that Christ has for us, we wouldn't come. We would be trying to see the new through the old man's eyes it's impossible. We can't follow the new holding on to the old, it's impossible. For in our hearts then Christ died for nothing the creator of man, allowed his creation to put him to death that's called love! AMEN

"THE SOUND OF THE GRINDING IS LOW"

Ecc 12:4: The sound of the grinding is low.

Rev 18 :22: The sound will be heard no more in you. The sound of the mill will be heard in you no more v 23 and the light the lamp will shine in you no more, and The Voice of the bridegroom and bride will be heard in you no more!

The sound of the grinding is low, slowing down. Of the mill be heard in you no more, due to the voice of the bridegroom and bride that were not hearing from God anymore. For the light of our lamb has gone out with in us. We once were the grinding mill, grinding out the corn, the meal, the grain, the seed of the word of God. Breaking down the word or the wheat of the word, so that we can make a spiritual loaf of bread to feed the hungry, those who hungering and we're thirsty to be fed from off God's table, has come to a halt, due to no one is hungering after the word of life and having gone their own way. Walking in the Darkness of their hearts. having 20/20 vision but spiritually blind and cannot see a far-off nor want to, let me eat my own bread.

Isa 4:1: We will eat our own bread, only let us be called by your name, take away are reproach.

Isa 3:10: They shall eat the fruit of their deeds. God is waiting if we want to know him. We go to a restaurant and read the menu, then order a menu We go to church read the menu, but don't partake in the meal, the meal is the meet, the corn, the fruit of God's word. Taste and see that God is good. When we taste we partake and when we partake now we're convicted. Conviction can taste very good, that leads us to Christ. Conviction and tastes very bad and we run from Christ. His word it's not tasting good to our palette or the doing of what we have heard does not come to pass. We turn from, run from truth, and seemingly the further away from God we get the better We feel. "Feeling is not a distance with God." we feel further from God, but he is on the present, has been and always will be there for us. He came for sinners he will be there for sinners, He died for sinners. if we have any hope at all, it's all in Christ, in Christ alone. Our Savior and Redeemer, our Friend and Father. Job said, "If I go to heaven, or go to hell you are there. There is no place to run, or to hide from God that he does not see. AMEN

"THE BENEFIT OF WEAKNESS"

There's a Benefit to Weakness, causing us to drop to are knees in submission, that we cannot know our way without Him.

Isaiah 57:15: I Dwell in the high and holy place, and also with him who is of a contrite and lowly spirit, to revive the spirit of the lowly, and to revive the heart of the contrite.

Isaiah 58:11: The Lord will guide you continually and satisfy your desire in scorching places and make your bones strong, and you shall be like a watered Garden, like a spring of water whose water do not fail.

Isaiah 60:1: Rise, shine for your light has come, and the glory of the Lord has risen upon You.

Isaiah 60:19: The sun shall be no more your light by day, nor for brightness shall the Moon give you light, but the Lord Will Be your everlasting light and your God will be Your Glory. V21 The branch of my planting, the work of My Hands, that I might be Glorified. AMEN

"THE JOY SET BEFORE HIM"

II Corinthians 5:12: For OUR SAKE He made Him to be SIN who knew NO SIN.

Hebrews 12:2: Who for the JOY that was set before Him endured the Cross.

It took Christ who knew NO SIN, to remove our Sin. Who for the JOY that was set before Him? What Joy was set before him? "US" who He formed, created, and breathed into us the Breath of Life. Our fall caused Him to come, because He Loves US. He did not want to be separated from Us, Sin separated. What parent wouldn't jump into the ocean to save their toddler that fell overboard in shark-infested waters. Sin is our shark-infested water and Jesus jumped into this world to Save Us. We're all drowning. Jesus IS our Life Jacket, who will put Him On?

Psalm 33:12: Blessed is the nation whose God is the Lord, the PEOPLE whom He Has Chosen As His Heritage!

"THE BATTLE IS IN THE MIND"

The Battle is in our mind, our minds have not been converted, After we have been saved, and come into this newness of Life. Then knowledge will be Pleasant to your soul. Understanding will guide you. Discretion will watch over you. For the knowledge of his word has been made known to us, to keep us on the path of life! Delivering us from the way of evil. There is another way if we choose that path. Some Forsaken the path of uprightness who walk in the way of Darkness, who Delight in the perverseness of evil men, whose path are crooked and who are Devious in their ways. You will be delivered from The Forbidden woman from the adulteress with her smooth words, you who are saved and seeking after God.

Proverbs 7:6: For from the window of her house "Satan" she looks out through the lattice and has seen Among the simple, among the Young a young Christians newly saved, lacking sense. Passing along her corner, taking the path to her house. In the Twilight, in the evening at the time of darkness and night. "Not in midday." She, Satan is loud, and at every street corner she lies in wait. She seizes him, she seeks Him eagerly and says, "I have found you. Come my husband is not at home he has taken a long journey." With her smooth talk she compels him. He follows her, as an ox goes to the slaughter, until an arrow pierces his Liver he "Does not know" that it will cost him his Life. Prov 2:19: none who go to her comeback, they do not regard the path of life. Once her Arrow Pierces our Spiritual liver we lose discernment from right and wrong, and Anything Goes. Our natural body, are natural liver, purifies our natural blood that we sustain life. When Satan's Dart strikes our Spiritual Liver, we lose Discernment of right and wrong. No longer able to discern Spiritual things, Spiritual matters of true Life. Now we're left to ourselves, without any spiritual Direction. AMEN.

"I AM THE DOOR, THE GAIT"

John 10:9: I am the door. if anyone enters by Me, he will be saved.

Psalm 16:11" You make known to me the path of Life. "Or You have shown me."

All will be shown few will enter! We are shown through the nudging of our God-given conscience. As quick as it comes in, we kick it out. This truth, this life, is not for me. No way am I going to help Noah build this boat, in this desert where it's never rained, you must be crazy. Talk about a waste of My Time, building something that's never going to be put to use. I've got better things to do with MY TIME.

Job 12:24: He takes away understanding from the Chiefs of the people of the Earth. Then what are we left with, Self!

Job 13: Will it be well with you when he searches you out?

Job 14:4: Who can bring a clean thing out of and unclean? There is no one.

Job 11:20: The way of escape will be lost to them, their hope is to breathe their last.

While banging on the sides of the Ark begging for entrance!

"THRASHING FLOOR"

Our heart is the threshing floor, what needs beaten out of us?

What has remained that we have not dealt with that God brings to his threshing floor. The threshing floor is a place of breaking down and revealing, and being exposed for what we are. A place that all will go through, to become the Bread that feeds the starving world for the Word of God.

"HIS WAYS ARE PAST FINDING OUT"

Romans 11:33: His ways are past finding out. What are we finding out in this life?

Job 38:1: The Lord answered job out of the Whirlwind and said, "Who is this that darkens Council by words without knowledge? I will question you, and you make it known to Me." Where were you Job when I laid the foundation of the Earth? Tell me, if YOU have understanding.

Job 38: 1-41, 39:1-30, 40:1-34, 42:1-17: "God's Wisdom past finding out."

Who Has put understanding in the inward parts Or given understanding to the mind? Is it by Your understanding that the hawk soars? Is it at Your command that the eagle Mounds up and makes his nest on high? The Lord answer job and said, "Address for action like a man, I will question you, and you make it known to Me." Will you ever put me in the wrong? Will you condemn Me that you may be in the right? The Hope of man is False.

Job answered the Lord and said, "I know that you can do all things. I have uttered what I did not understand, things to wonderful for me, which I did not know. I have heard of you by the hearing of the ear, but now my eyes see You."

His ways our paths finding out, meaning we will never come to the full understanding, the full knowledge of God in this life. Yet, while we live what are we finding out about God, His truth, His word, His life. That He will reveal to Us, IF we seek, IF we knock, He Will Answer. AMEN

"HELP YOU SEE YOUR NEED FOR ME"

I orchestrated circumstances and events in your life to help you see your need for me, my way of calling you.

The word wants us to conform.

God's purpose is not connected to our age, it's connected to our faith.

Never despise the day of small things.

There is more grace in God's heart, then sinning our past.

People cannot give us what we need, only God can give us what we need.

If you don't bump into Satan on this journey, it's because you're both headed in the same direction.

Yesterday's faith never seems to carryover to tomorrow's problems.

Divine revelation is to guide man.

This book the Bible will keep you from sin and sin will keep you from this book.

The Lord weighs the motives of the heart.

I am deaf to what you say until you give me reason to listen.

To whom much is given much will be required.

Bitterness only consumes the container that holds it.

Obey God and leave all the consequences to him.

His word Define Who We Are.

You know, we can have a substitute for God, it's called the world.

The Bible it's not like a refrigerator, nothing in there goes bad.

Don't let the voice of God be silenced and you.

When we are at our weakest God is strongest.

If we move away from the truth, we become less than a noise.

Is your comfort, keeping you from your calling?

Where our joy comes from, will determine when it runs out.

Abide in me and I'll abide in you.

If our emotions control our Joy it will run out.

Our joy should not be connected to things that cannot sustain us.

Every Secret of my heart shall be made known.

What's happening to me is nothing compared to what's happening in me.

God word is a two-edged sword, that cuts and heels at the same time.

Your identity will be tied to whatever you give your heart to.

Every day I wake up, it's my will, or his will.

We give up first in our mind, and then the flesh follows.

It's boring, and inconvenient, and getting in my way, Christianity.

Don't compare ourselves with someone else, walk-in your gifting. Let God use what he has put in US.

The Creator, coming to the created.

Love has a name it's, commitment and understanding.

Wherever there's a potential of love, there is potential of pain.

What void are we trying to fill?

It doesn't matter how well we do what we do. if we don't do what we're supposed to do.

God can use our faithfulness who directed us to the real role which HE has called us to.

You give anybody who's looking for a way out, and they'll take it.

If I have a problem giving forgiveness, I'll have a problem receiving forgiveness.

If you want to have faith that moves mountains. first you need faith that moves you.

Harden not your heart.

What speech to us the loudest, the world or God.

Don't own them, they own you, the things of the world.

The important thing is how big is God to you.

Your sermon is not in your mouth, it's in your pain.

We imitate when we can't be real.

We're not in trapped by Who We Are. we are trapped by who we think we are.

God Whispers to us in our pleasure, he speaks to us in our conscience, but shouts to us in our pain. pain is God's megaphone.

God's pulling me out of the common, and making me uncommon.

Don't let, don't allow the voice of limitation stop you from doing what the Lord has called you to do.

You can't trust God if you don't know God loves you.

Our identity will be attached to whatever our heart is.

Every day is a second chance.

Nothing builds character and a person more than trouble.

Our flesh wants to pull us to the very thing that Christ has redeemed us from. our flesh wants to be in control again.

We are to take our thoughts captive.

In whom much is given much is required.

To some first Flirtation and then the fall.

Hope deferred makes the heart sick.

The Lord can restore the years the Locust have eaten.

II CORINTHIANS 4:4 THE GOD OF THIS WORLD

The god of this world has blinded the minds of the unbelievers, to keep them from seeing the Light of the gospel of the Glory of Christ! We have a HEART and that's what satan Is After. He's got our mind. The god of this age Has Blinded the minds. But God through his Mercy and His Love for us has also given us a Heart. Our Heart is the way out, the way through a blinded mind. We cannot see with our mind, we see with our Heard.

Our heart is the Open Door, the way out of darkness into His Glorious Light and Life. Through His Love for us, will we walk through the door He has provided for us, the Only Way, the Only Door, Jesus Christ.

Revelation 3:8: I have set before you an Open Door, which no one is able to Shut. v 13 He who has an ear, let him hear, V 22

Jesus made His Call to us, from the Cross, Forgive Them For They Do Not Know What They do.

AMEN

"IF ANYONE THIRST"

John 7:37,39: Jesus cried out, "If anyone thirst, let him come to me and drink. For out of His heart will flow rivers of Living Water." This He said about the spirit, of those who believed in Him where to receive. For as yet the Spirit had not been given, because Jesus was not yet glorified or broken, to be poured out on All Flesh. AMEN

"PREPARE SUPPER FOR ME"

Luke 17:7,10: Will anyone of you who has a servant plowing or keeping sheep say to him when he has come in from the field, come at once and recline at my table? Will he not rather say to him, prepare supper for me, while I eat and drink, and afterwards you will eat and drink? Does he thank the servant because he did what was commanded? So you also, when you have done all that you were commanded, say, we are unworthy servants, we have only done what was our duty.

Will He "God" not rather say to him, or meaning" us today." Prepare supper for me and serve me, while I eat and drink While God eats and drinks. Is God eating and drinking and feeding off what we have done this day. While working in his field that he gave us to work in, and has equipment us to do. Prepare supper for me. God is all ears in waiting to hear from us while seated at his table, waiting to be served. Well God, I thank you for my health that I can get out and serve you. Thank you for the witness today to that young man wanting to hear from you. And answered prayer for Mary and able to breathe better. Thank you for road safety, watching over my family and protecting them, and thank you that my car started that I can get out. Thank you for the field that you have called me to work in. Then, afterwards, we will eat and drink off of God's table. While he talks to us through his word and meditating on him, and giving us revelation that we might feed on.

Luke 1: 53: He has filled the hungry with good things and the rich he has sent away empty.

Prov 10:3: The Lord does not let the righteous go hungry.

Prov 10:21: The lips of the righteous feed many but fools die for lack of sense.

So after we have done all that we were commanded say, "We are unworthy servants, we have only done that was our duty." God is listening and waiting to hear from us. even though he knows everything, he wants to hear from his creation, God has ears to AMEN

"PROUD HEART, NO ROOM"

Luke 2:7: And she gave birth to her" first born" son and wrapped him in swaddling clothes and laid him in a Manger, because there was no room for him in the inn.

No room in the inn. There's No room in a proud heart to give birth to Christ in our lives, He will go someplace else, where He's welcomed. A humble and holy Manger, a humble and contrite heart God will not despise, Birth will take place, and all around will notice!

To know Truth is to experience it! It's not head knowledge, it's Heart relationship. Our minds need transformed every day.

I Peter 3:15: Always be prepared to give an answer to everyone who asked you, give the reason for the hope that is in you.

"SPIRITUAL FOOD THAT SUSTAINS"

Spiritual food that sustains, strengthens the Spiritual body. Come and buy, wine and milk, bread, without money without price.

God provision for our Spirit is bought by "Faith" and Faith alone. Faith is the economy of God. He who has ten talents went and got another ten. He who had I talent did by Faith nothing with it.

The story of the Father and his two Sons. Which one did the will of his Father, the one who Did, are we doing?

"GOD GIVEN ABILITY"

God has given us all an ability, it's what we Do with His ability that one day He can say welcome in good and Faithful Servant. I may not have the ability to do ten and God knows that. But if He gives me two along with the two that God has given, "Comes the ability" the enablement, strength, will, drive, provision, working out to gain another two, which is doubled then what I have started with. Which all is God's we have nothing to boast about, nothing to proclaim, not even to shout about when it's all Him working through us! Something that we could never accomplish on our own. "So where is boasting then, it is excluded." To Him goes the Glory, the Praise, and Honor. To Him goes the thankfulness because it all comes from Him, His Might, His Power, His Revelation, His Working. That were just a vessel that have availed ourselves for God to work through, work in and establish Himself in us. God is looking for a willing Heart, a willing Mind which has been conformed to His image. To work through us. So where is boasting then, it is excluded, it's All in Him, about Him, through Him. Because of a broken and a contrite Heart that God can work through. His ways are beyond finding out, limitless, unending, beyond the Highest Height, the Deepest depth, and Wider than the widest breath. There we find the Beginning of God and His workings, up on this planet we call Earth. AMEN

"Through the Knowledge of him who "Called Us"

II Peter 1:3: His Divine power as granted to us all things that pertain to life and godliness, through the" Knowledge of Him" who called us to his own Glory and excellence.

Psalm 16:11: "You Make Known To Me" the Path Of Life.

Psalm 32:8: I will instruct you and teach you in the way you should go. We did not find the Path Of Life on our own. Some find the Path of Life easier than others. Not letting their intellect hinder them, let Faith Arise then our eyes will be open. Without Faith We remain Blind.

Through the "Knowledge" of him who called us! All things that pertain to Life and Godliness Through the" Knowledge" of Him. How well do We Know Him? Knowing Christ comes from the Heart, not our Minds. Therefore, everyone is equal all having the same ability to approach His throne. Our pride will stop Us from approaching His Throne, we are left to Ourselves.

"Everyone shall be Equal," like the celebration of booths from the Old Testament. Right, Poor, Old, Young, All living outside In the Elements, as the Israelites did for forty years in the desert. A reminder of God's provision, lest we Forget. Rich, or Poor, Intelligent and not so smart, All Exposed TO and enduring the same.

Psalm 32:8: I will instruct you and teach you in the way which you should go I will counsel you with my eye upon you. AMEN

"WAITING"

Waiting can frustrate Us, bother us, cause us to worry, get upset, seemingly put a delay in our life, could discourage us, cause us to Lose hope.

Waiting is in the time zone, which The Flesh lives in. Our spirit is eternal, just like God who gave it. Waiting Works a purpose in US, if we do not learn from it, it will be repeated. Waiting test are character, waiting can Define Who We Are. We may not show frustration to others or being discouraged, but it can lie in our innermost being and one day come out. Waiting needs to be dealt with while we wait. We're to check our countenance for truly what is on the inside of us will come out. We're to deal with it before it takes root, which it will if not dealt with. God is draining off the dross daily as we go on to perfection. Embrace it our God of everything knows what He is doing, not us. So, rejoice and be glad that pure love which we will not understand until we go to be with Him. He loves His creation that's why we are even here. We're not to think highly of ourselves, least we become puffed up, and pay the price of waiting which rubs us wrong, which was only meant for our good. He directs our path, He leads us, not we ourselves. Lest we become dull of hearing, lacking in vision followed by leaning on our understanding. Going back to what we have been delivered from! And wanting to go back to Egypt where we seemingly had it better, at least we were in control somewhat…

Wait is Mentioned in the Bible 154 times, I wonder why?

Waiting teaches us to walk in His ways. Abraham had to wait on God and Look what happened.

Isaiah 40:31: They who Wait for the Lord Shall renew their strength, they Shall Mount up with wings like eagles, they Shall run and not be weary, they Shall walk and not faint.

Psalm 27:14: Wait for the Lord, be strong, and Let Your Heart Take courage, Wait for the Lord!

II Peter 3:8: Do not overlook this one fact, that with the Lord one day is a thousand years, and a thousand years as one day.

If God makes Us Wait it's for Glory.

Isaiah 30:18" Blessed are all those who Wait for Him. AMEN

ISAIAH 43:2

When You pass through the waters, I will be with you, and through the rivers, they shall Not overwhelm you. When you walk through Fire you shall not be burned, and the Flame shall Not consume You.

When we pass through the Waters, the Rivers, through the Fire and the Flames. It's inevitable, these Waters, Rivers, Flames, Will come for He said, When You "Pass Through" I will be with You." We're being tested, tried, and proven. AMEN

How firm a foundation, you Saints of the Lord, is laid for YOUR FAITH in his excellent word! What more can he say then to you he has said, to you who for Refuge to Jesus has fled? When through the deepest Waters I call You To Go, the rivers of Sorrow shall not overflow, for I will be with you, your trouble to bless. When through fiery trials your pathway Shall Lie. My grace all sufficient, shall be your supply. The flames cannot hurt you. My Only desire that your Dross be consume, and Your Gold to Refine. AMEN

JOHN 14:6

Jesus said I am the Way, the Truth, and the Life. No one comes to the father except through Me.

"Jesus is the way out of our Sin, the Truth in this life that we live, and the Life in the everlasting."

JOHN 10:27

Jesus said My Sheep hear My Voice, and I "Know Them," and they follow Me.

"I can't make you here. Jesus said, "My Sheep Hear My Voice"

"We gave Him the cross, not knowing we gave Him a throne!"

WAIT

Wait? God himself had to wait nine months. There's a process we go through learning his ways. We as a baby cannot abort itself. But we can abort ourselves from being like Christ. Let patience have her perfect work. We're not microwave Christians, God is baking us and his oven. Heat upon Heat, Test, up on Test, Line upon Line, here a little they're a little. Kindergarten, grade school, Junior High, High School, college. Then the real education of life, this does not happen overnight. To be used we must become a servant, ready to be stepped on to help others.

Proverbs 3: My son, do not forget my teachings, but let your heart keep my Commandments, for length of days and years of life and peace they will add to you. Let not steadfast love and faithfulness forsake you, bind them around your neck, write them on the tablet of your heart. You will find favor and good success in the sight of God and man. Trust in the Lord with all your heart, and do not lean on your own understanding. In all your ways acknowledge Him, and He will make straight your paths. Be not wise in your own eyes, fear the lord, and turn away from evil. It will be help to your flesh and refreshment to your bones. Honor the Lord with your wealth and with the first of all your produce. Then your barns will be filled with plenty, and your vats will be bursting with wine. My son do not despise the Lord's discipline or be weary of his reproof, Lord reproves him whom He loves, As father the Son and whom he Delights. Blessed is the one who finds wisdom, and the one who gets understanding, for the gain from her is better than gain from Silver and her prophet better than gold. Long life is in her right hand, and her left hand are riches and honor. Her ways are ways of pleasantness, and all her paths our peace. She is a tree of life to those who lay hold on her, those who hold her fast are called blessed. The Lord by wisdom founded the Earth, by understanding he established the heavens, by his knowledge the depths broke up and the clouds drop down the Dew. My son, do not lose sight of these keep sound wisdom and discretion, and they will be life for your soul. Then you will walk on your way securely, and your foot will not stumble. Do not withhold good from those to whom it is due, when it is in your power to do it. The wise will inherit honor, but fools get disgrace. AMEN

"WISDOM"

Romans 8:31: What, then, shall we say in response to this? If God is for us, "Who can be against us?" Question, who can be against us? Our Mind, Our Flesh, Our Will, Our Feet Going In The Wrong Direction, Our Lust, Our Eyes. That's the wrong direction. We are not an Island unto ourselves.

God said about Adam it is not good for man to live alone. Today we have the Spirit, we have the Comforter, we have Christ with Us, we're not alone.

God's word, where to read it, memorize it, think upon it. If we only do this, and Not Speak It, we have just Build Ourselves Another BARN.

Luke 12:16,21 "So is the one who lays up Treasures for himself and is not rich toward God."

"JOHN 1:1 IN THE BEGINNING WAS THE WORD"

In the beginning was the WORD and the WORD was with God and the WORD "WAS GOD." The WORD WAS GOD. And the WORD became FLESH and dwelled among us. God did not send a substitute to fulfill what HE Spoke. He GOD came Himself, born of a woman, just like you and me. His name is called Emmanuel, meaning GOD WITH US. Taking on the Name of Jesus while God was here in the Flesh. God is a title, Jesus is the name that, at the Name of JESUS, every knee shall bend and every tongue shall confess that JESUS Is Lord. Father it is finished, the work in the flesh is done. I AM going back home and take up who I AM in the Spirit, what I was before I came. My flesh, My blood was needed to buy your Salvation, Perfect Blood, not born under the curse of the fall of Adam. Which cleanses and sets free those under the curs that believe. He who spoke the Law into existence came and fulfiled It HIMSELF, in the flesh of Jesus Christ Emmanuel, God With us, That He experienced in the Flesh what he made Adam. John 14:9,10: Whoever has seen Me has Seen the Father. I am in the Father and the Father is in ME. AMEN

JOHN 15:13

Greater Love has no one then this, that someone lay down his life for his friend.

To lay down one's life, that's laying down Self, Ego, Strength, Wisdom, that's Beneath me to lose my life that much. We've been called to lay down our lives. If naturally I lay down my life, then my future witness, effectiveness in this life is gone. If I die to sells, then others can live. Pick up our cross and follow where self cannot go. Behold I show you a new way, a new way where we do not need are natural eyes, God wants us to see with the eyes our heart now. We may have 20/20, vision before we got Saved, but in God's eyes we were still blind. Having ears but not hearing, what the Spirit is saying, not natural hearing. Another way, we're to live and move and have our being. A Peace of heaven here on Earth is losing self. Self is going back to the Dust. That's why we are not to think highly of oneself, that's just how it IS. There's no stopping that which is coming for our flesh, we're all the same. Some smarter, some Richer, some stronger, but ALL going the same place, the grave. It's the new man, the new person that God has forgiven, that He will take with him when He returns. From out of the grave to heaven, or while we have breath in our lungs. In a Twinkle of an eye it will be finished, no time to get ready then, it's too late, We've missed our train. He who's train fills the temple says for the Last Time, Father it is Finished! It's rolled up like a scroll, done, complete, finished. AMEN

"THOUGHTS"

Amos 6:1: Woe to those who are at ease in Zion.

Amos 8:11: Behold, the days are coming declares the Lord God, when I will send a famine on the land, not a famine of bread, not a thirst for water, but of Hearing the word of the Lord.

Amos 7:7: this is what he showed me, behold, the Lord was standing beside a wall built with a Plumb line, with a Plumb line in his hand.

Obadiah 1:15: The day of the Lord is near upon All Nations. As you have Done, it will be Done to You, your Deeds shall return on your own head.

Obadiah 1:3: The pride of your heart has deceived you.

Yes, we are to live, and move, and have our being in Him. There are Times when we Wait. Waiting on God's will. God's timing, is perfect. Otherwise, we will do our thing. Like the children of Israel, they could not Wait for Moses to come down off the mountain. So, they went and made a golden calf, to worship! With God or without God we all worship something. Choose you this day who you will serve, there is no gray area, Life or Death.

"TESTIMONY"

I was saved about nine months, and I asked the Lord, if there was an eleventh commandment what would have it said?

He said, "Thou shall not sweat it!" I've given you ten and you can't keep those, why would I give you an eleventh. By Faith do what you know to do.

I came home from work, and walking up the front walk, between my house and the neighbor's house. Just as quick as you can blink, there was a ladder going from the ground, up through the clouds. I blinked my eyes and look again, and it was gone. What was spoken to me was, which rung on the ladder is the most important. I thought Within Myself and thought the top run Meaning you have achieved. You have made it. Before those words came out of my mouth, I said no. I said out loud the Bottom Rung, if that's what I'm to be the Bottom Rung that I can help other people on the ladder onto the second rung that would be my portion.

ISAIAH 35

The wilderness and the dry land shall be glad, and the desert shall blossom as the rose. It shall blossom abundantly and rejoice with joy and singing. The glory of Lebanon shall be given to it, Strengthen the weak hands, and make firm the feeble knees. Then the eyes of the blind shall be opened, and the ears of the deaf unstopped. Then shall the lame men leap like a deer, and the tongue of the mute sing for joy. For waters break forth in the wilderness, and streams in the desert. The thirsty ground springs of water. A highway shall be there, and it shall be called the Way of Holiness, the unclean shall not pass over it. It shall belong to those who walk on the way, but the redeemed shall walk there. They shall obtain gladness and joy, and sorrow and sighing, shall flee away. We are the wilderness, the dry ground, the desert, "Before We Got Saved," That was "Us" without, Hope, Dry, Barron, Desolate, Blind, no ears to hear, no flowing Water, no Stream. But thinking we had it made. Until we heard that still Quite voice, come and follow Me. Then everything Changed. When the Water from Heaven flows Growth happens, Eyes Open, Deaf Ears now hear, the mute tongue Speaks, and You "Know" How It Happened ! AMEN

"ROMANS 12:2 BE NOT CONFORMED"

Be not conformed to this world, but be Transformed by the Renewing out of your MIND. As Christians our spirit has been saved, redeemed. Now that were saved, we are to transform, renew "Our Mind," which is Not saver, there is where the battle takes place for our Eternal Life, until we go to our grave. Jesus says "Do You Love Me? Then don't cheat on Me.

We renew our minds through the Word Daily, least our mind takes over, Rises up against the spirit whereby we have been saved, redeem, renewed, cleansed and forgiven. We are to transform our Minds, the Lord has redeemed our Spirit. We have been redeemed from the fall of our parents, Adam and Eve. Through our Faith in repenting of our sins. When Adam and Eve were removed from the Garden of Eden, due to their transgression, so were we. Now that we have been forgiven, and cleansed from our fallen nature, we have been made new. Now we are to renew our Minds Daily. Just like we get dressed every morning put on our clothes to cover our flesh. Were to put on our robe of righteousness, our Garment given to us by God. Least our mind Rises up and says put me on today. That which we have been redeemed from that which wants to rise up against and Control Us speaking to us, without saying an Audible word, our mind becomes louder, stronger, easier to be listen to then the voice the word of God.

Joshua 24:13,15: I give You a Land on which You have not Labored and Cities that you have not Built, You Eat the Fruit of the vineyard and Olive Orchards that You did not Plant. Are we not Satisfied with what God has done for us! Choose You This Day Who You Will Serve!" Our Mind or Our Spirit. AMEN

TONGUES

Genesis 11:1-9: The Tower of Babel

Genesis 11:1 says that the whole earth had one language, and everyone used the same words.

Saying come let us build ourselves a city and a tower, with its top in the heavens and let us make a name for ourselves.

The Lord came down and said that they are one people, and that they all have one language. "Let us go down there to confuse their language so that they won't be able to understand one another's speech."

There was only one earthly language.

So, God came down and confused the language, their speech, so they couldn't build.

The New Testament and tongues now.

A Heavenly Language, a language from God, pure in speech for the building up of His Kingdom.

Not ourselves, as was building of the tower of Babel.

They said, "Let us make a name for ourselves."

God wasn't involved in that, so He came down.

Now we've been given a heavenly language for the building up and edifying of the Church.

I Corinthians 14:4, "The one who speaks in a tongue builds up himself."

And in verse 18, "I thank God that I speak in tongues more than all of you."

Paul said if I speak in tongues of men and of angels, but have not love, I am a noisy gong or a clanging cymbal.

Like in the building of the tower of Babel, which was done wrong, we can mess up the pure language of God.

Our pride, our vanity, and our wisdom all get in the way of God's building.

"GREATER WORKS"

John 14:12: Truly I say to you, whoever believes in Me will also do the works that I do, and greater works than these will he do, because I am going to the Father, The greater work is when someone gets Saved. They are brought from Death to Life.

Eternal Life, never to die. Jesus rose the dead only to die again. When someone gets Saved, Spiritual there raised never to die again, this is the Greater Work, I feel through Christ. AMEN

"GOD'S NAME IS JESUS"

John 17:6: I have manifested Your Name to the people whom you gave me out of the world.

v 10 Keep them in Your Name You have given Me. v 12 while I was with them, I kept them in Your Name which You have given Me v 26 I made known to them Your Name. Matt 1:20

An Angel of the Lord appeared to Joseph in a dream saying She Mary will bear a son, and you shall call His Name Jesus. v 23 Behold, the virgin shall conceive and bear a Son, and they shell call HIS name Immanuel, meaning God with up. Now the Prophet have long time all passed away.

Zechariah 14:9: The Lord will be king over all the earth, On that day the Lord will be one and his Name ONE. Knowing that Immanuel was coming, meaning God with us. But not knowing that His Name would be Jesus. Where all power in heaven and earth is given, In thought word or deed, do All in the Name of Jesus. Am I, are we leaving God out? No Jesus is God, Immanuel God with us!

Isaiah 9:6: For to us a child is born, to us a Son is given, and the government shall be upon His shoulders, and His Name shall be called Wonderful, Counselor, Mighty God, Everlasting Father, Prince of Peace. All these titles are summed up in the Name of Jesus.

He Is All In All. The name of Jesus covers all these attributes.

Malachi 2:2 If you will not listen, if you will not take it to heart to give honor to My Name, says the Lord of hosts, then I will send the curse upon you and I will cures your blessing, because you have not lay it to heart.

Zechariah 14:9: On THAT DAY the Lord will be One and His Name ONE.

Isaiah 52:6: There for My People shall know My Name! "We Have TO be His People to Know His NAME. I knew the Name Jesus, before I got Saved, but only in Name. He was someone else's Father not mine. I had no relationship with Him, He was not my Father, though He wanted to be. Immanuel, God With Us and I missed it for years. Now He is My Father, I know Him and He knows ME.

John 1:12: Who Believed in "His Name," He gave the right to become children of God. AMEN

STATISTIC

Nine percent of church-going Christians read their Bible.

The word of life, Living Waters, The Well of salvation, the stream of life, whose water fail not. Rivers whose water gives Life. It's the word of God, drink by reading and believing or go thirsty. My people perish for the lack of wisdom, drink and be satisfied.

"WHY HAVE YOU FORSAKEN ME"

My God, my God, why have you forsaken me. God cannot look on sin. While the sins of the world were placed upon His body, God turned away.

Three hours of Darkness upon the whole land, the Earth quaked And the Veil was torn from top to bottom. To where all can enter in now it's not only the high priest. This has been done away with by the death of Jesus Christ, the Veil being torn in two, through believing, we enter and now, salvation, born again, behold all things become new, By and through Faith.

We may have a head knowledge of Christ, but not a heart relationship!

THE PRODIGAL SON LUKE 15:11

So, the younger son said to his father, "Father, give me what's coming to me."

And his father did.

And then the son went on his journey.

But he had already taken a journey in his heart - away from God.

We don't have to physically take a journey away from God to feel that we have distanced ourselves from Him.

But in our heart of hearts, we would rather be doing something else.

Actually, our journey has already begun away from God without leaving.

The scriptures tell us that not many days later the younger son gathered all that he had and took a journey to a far country.

He was just going to a place where his heart had already gone to.

That he took all that he had, but nothing to help him on this journey.

He'd had enough of that and left that at home, pushing it back deep down in his heart.

Once you've tasted that God is good, you cannot bury it (though we may try.)

In the far country, he squandered his portion in reckless living (anything away from God is reckless.)

There is no bigger sin little sin all is darkness there's no gray area.

God measures sin all worthy of separation.

the same repentance brings the seeming smaller sin or large sin back into order back into you're forgiven.

it's not I've sent so bad for so long that we think that a long repentance shows that I am sorry repenting and turning from shows your heart along time singing is our time or our schedule in Gods there's no length of time we repent and move on forgiven God lives where there is no time, you're forgiven there's no yesterday or tomorrow with God it's right now forever.

Now, when he had spent all in not until he had spent all then a severe mighty famine arose in that land that land was his heart, and he began to be in need the beginning of maybe I should return to my father and go back home, but his pride self ego at this point would not let him.

So, he went and hired himself out to one of the citizens of that country, who sent him to his fields to feed the pigs.

Now there came a mighty famine in the land, the nature physical land.

Why would he be feeding the pigs the husk of the corn that the pigs did eat? And he himself.

Someone is eating the corn that the pigs are feeding on the husk he would have in vain filled his belly with the husk of the corn.

If there's a mighty famine in the natural, how could there be corn to eat let alone any pigs to feed?

They would have been slaughtered and eaten to stay off a natural famine when the real famine was in the heart, and no one gave him anything No one gave him anything because they had nothing to give him nothing spiritual like he had back home that he left now he was in want and coming to himself finally.

For he was perishing here with hunger for the bread of his father's words a drink from his father's fountain of living water around like minded people not here in this foreign land where the word of my father is not heard or welcome when he finally came to himself, he said how many of my father's hired servants have more than enough bread, but I perish here in hunger.

I will go to my father I will say to him, "Father, I have sinned against heaven and before you."

God sees everything. "I am no longer worthy to be called your son."

He arose and went to his father.

And when he was still a long way off, his father saw him.

How far is a long way off? We may feel that we are a long way off, a long time away from God, but there's no distance with God When we repent, we are there back right with the father no yes and no time for given the father ran and fell upon his neck giving him a hug to welcome him home, his son never repented to his father at this time the son's repentance had already taken place! That's why he came home.

Repentance had already taken place in his heart and his father welcomed him.

Putting on his best robe, the ring back on his finger, and shoes on his feet, the father killed the fated calf.

"Let's eat and celebrate for my son was dead and is alive again!

He was lost and is found!"

They began to celebrate.

Now the older son was out in the field, but not the field as plowing with an ox.

The older son was coming in from his field of ministering. Preaching and teaching his father's word.

When he came in from the field and drew near to the house, he heard music and dancing.

He called to one of the servants and asked what these things meant.

"Well, your brother has come home, and your father has killed the fattened calf because he has received him back safe and sound."

But the older son was angry and refused to go in.

Father came out and entreated him God himself but he answered his father look as if his father did not know

"These many years I have served you and I never disobeyed your command. Yet you never gave me the fated calf that I might celebrate with "my friends", separation here between himself his friends and God

The older son never got the fattened calf because there was an area in his heart that needed taken care of and it came to full circle with his brother coming back home the older son was doing his father's will and never breaking the commandments but his heart was" never really in it" when he said you never gave me the fattened calf that I might make merry with my friends why the separation of himself and his friends, but jealousy in me wanting to leave to go but never did.

Just look at my brother this son of yours after coming back and having devoured what you have given him with prostitutes. I never read anything about the younger brother wasting his inheritance on prostitutes.

how that slipped out of the older brother's mouth because it was in his heart what he would have done he said look all these years I have worked for you oh the exposure of the heart yes something God already knows about because he is God Amen

"LUKE 5:15,19 WHAT IN OUR LIVES THAT NEED TORN UP?"

Great crowds gathered to hear Jesus and to be healed of their infirmities. on one day as he was teaching, Pharisees and teachers of the law were sitting there, the power of the Lord was with him to heal, and behold some men were bringing on a bed a man who was paralyzed, and they were seeking to bring him in and lay him before Jesus. Finding no way to bring him in, because of the crowd they went up on the roof, removing some tiles to make an opening and lower him on a stretcher through the roof, into the midst of the crowd before Jesus.

Are there areas in our lives that need Torn Up in order to receive what we are praying for? They had a hope, a desire, a belief, if they could only get to Jesus, "But something was in their way," What Stop Us? What needs to be removed in our walk with Christ, what needs Torn Up Before we come to Jesus with our petition, our need? Jesus saw their faith transparent to us but a substance to Jesus AMEN

"LUKE 12:16-21 THE BARNS OF THE RICH MAN"

Jesus told them a parable saying. The land of a rich man produced plentiful, and he thought to Himself, what shall "I Do" for I have nowhere to store My Crops? He said, "I Will do this." "I Will" tear down My Barns and build larger ones, and there I Will store all My Grain and My Goods. I Will Say to My Soul, soul you have ample Goods laid up for many years, relax, eat, drink, and be merry. But God said to him, you fool! This night your soul is required of you, and the things you have prepared who's will they be? So is the one who lays up treasure for Himself and is not rich towards God.

The problem was, he thought to himself, nothing about Christ and his provision, or what the Lord has done for him, no thank you towards God at all! "Just me," I and self, what I Will Do! He thought what will I Do? I will tear down My Barns, I will store My grain And my goods, I will say to my soul, "Soul you have ample Goods laid up for many years. Relax, eat, drink, and be merry." But God said you fool, this night your soul is required of you.

"Our barns are our Hearts where we store up the true riches." Our testimony of coming to Christ is in there, wisdom and instruction of God's word, so we can lead a sinner to Christ so they can start their Barn being filled, THEIR HEART, if we endure to the end. Revelation of God's word, parables that's speak to us, answers to prayers, our struggles and trials, Are Rising and falling, times when we came short, but we persevered, enduring having hope. Believing and trusting and he who can do all things. He who is for us not against us. He who holds Us by his right hand. I Cor 2:7-14.

We impart a secret and hidden wisdom of God, which God decrease before the ages for our Glory. None of the rulers of this age understood this, for if they had, they would not have crucified the Lord of Glory. But it is written, what no eye has seen, nor ear heard, nor the heart of man imagined what God has prepared for those who love him. These things God has revealed to us through the spirit. For the spirit searches everything even the depths of God. No one comprehends the thoughts of God except the spirit of God. That we might understand the things freely given to us by God. We impart this in words not taught by human wisdom but taught by the spirit, interpreting spiritual truths to those who are spiritual. The natural person does not accept the things of the spirit of God, for they are folly to Him, and He is not able to understand them because they are spiritually discerned, There is no Barn to store The Riches of God. Our barn comes and starts after salvation, after conversion, believing, trusting and adhering to, that we can begin to fill our barns, Our HEARTS, given to us by Christ, where no rust, nor canker worm, moth can destroy. Now to occupy until I come. We will never be able to fill our barns with the true riches, for eye has not seen Nor Ear heard, nor the heart of man imagined what God has for those who love him. When I come back who will I find doing or who will I find Starting their Barn that can never be filled in this life. Occupy until I come, for God chose what is foolish in this world to shame the wise, Jesus has become to us the wisdom of God righteousness and sanctification and Redemption. What shape is your Barn, Your Heart In?

Ezekiel 28:2-5: Because your heart is proud, and you have said I am a god. Yet you are but a man, and no god, do you make your heart like the heart of a god? By your wisdom and your understanding, you have made wealth for yourself and have gathered gold and silver into your Treasures. But your great wisdom in your trade, you have increased your wealth, and your heart has become Proud in your wealth.

Luke 12:43: But blessed is that servant whom his master will find so doing the right things when he comes.

I Tim 6:19: Storing up Treasures for themselves as a good foundation for the future, so that they may take hold of that which is true life.

Prov 21:13: Whosoever closes his ear to the Cry of the poor will himself call and not be answered. This man kept what he had, chucked everything away in His Barn and lending nothing out to others, for he had worked long and hard for this. Only to build bigger barns to hold his seemingly wealth.

Jeremiah 9:23: Let not the wise man boast in his wisdom, let not the Mighty Man boast in his might, let not the rich man boast in his riches.

Prov 11:28: Whosoever trust in his riches will fall. This rich man in this parable, his land produce plentifully. The problem was that he thought to himself, "What shall I Do?" Which this man never consulted, he did not consider God in any of his decision making, he did it all on his own. He thought to himself, nothing about Christ in His provision, or what the Lord had done for him. No thank you towards God at all! Just me, myself, and I. He said I Will do this, I Will tear down My barns, I Will store My Grain and My Goods, I Will say to My Soul, so you have plenty Goods laid up for many years. Relax, eat, drink be merry. But God said you fool! this night your soul is required of you. You have laid up Treasures for Yourself, but are Not rich towards God.

Ezekiel 28: Because your heart is proud, by your wisdom and your understanding you have made wealth for yourselves and have gathered gold and silver into Treasures, but have not been rich towards God. You're only going to tear down and build more to store what you should have given away freely, for freely we receive and freely we give away that more may be given from above. AMEN

"LUKE 8:11-15 PARABLE OF THE SOWER OF THE SEED"

The seed is the word of God. The ones along the path are those who have heard the word of God, and before the word, which was heard, before it had taken place end their Hearts, before it had taken place in their makeup, our actions, before it even had a chance to change our thinking, even before we have understanding of the Word it's gone. So that we may not believe and be saved.

The ones on the rock, when they heard the word received the Word with joy. For what the word could do in their lives. But having no root, or a heart that would not Allow the word, which they heard to have its way in our lives. In that believing for a while, but when time of testing came, "The Test." You say that you got saved last night? What for? Do you realize what you are going to be missing out on? You have your whole life ahead of you. Christian now you're saying? you got saved? Saved from having a Good Time, come on now, come with us.

Job 5: 21: You shall be hidden from the Lash of the tongue. The word of God that fell among the thorns, they heard and as they go on Their Way. That's what we were doing, before hearing the word, going on Our Way. Then after hearing the word, we continue going Our Way, with no change, no effect in our life. Our way chokes the word we heard out of our life, we trample it under our feet, not knowing that the word which was bringing life to us, We have put to Death. We do have power, power to say no to the Word of God. Never thinking that you could trump God. Now for those who hearing the word, they hold on to it. Liking what they have heard, having understanding that this change in their life is needed. That they have walked their way to no end. Now having an honest heart before God.

Job 5:18: For He wounds but He binds up, He shatters But His hand heals. That the word they heard had broken a heart, that now can be

Broken. Broken now to heal a life, Broken to mend, Broken to fix, Broken that except and allows the newness of Life to come in.

Job 8:17: What is man that you make so much of Him and that you set your heart on Him. AMEN

"MATT 13:47-48 THE KINGDOM OF HEAVEN LIKE A NET"

The kingdom of heaven is like a net that was thrown into the sea, "the Sea of humanity." Gathering fish of every kind; Greeks, Jews, Chinese, Americans, Mexicans, Italian, Polish, Russian, and so on and so on. Gathering people of every race that got saved where in His Net the Kingdom Now. When it was full, or at the end of time, 'God's time' when it will be rolled up like a scroll. When it was full, no more being saved. When the Angels came down and sorted and separated the good from the bad Christian. Those who have done the will of God and those who pretended to be working in the Kingdom having no fruit. The very elect that have been led astray.

Matt 24:24: For false Christ and false prophets will rise and perform great signs and wonders, so as to lead astray if possible, even the elect.

Nature, God's creation, puts it this way. All the honey bees in the hive, and there are drone bees who do not gather honey, do not do any work, but they live and exist there. When winter comes the worker bees, those who have gathered honey for their very existence. When the cold weather sets in and around freezing time. Then the worker bees gather together and run out, push out, drive out the Drone Bees, and they freeze to death. Non-productive, no fruit, whose leaves weather end Fall Away. AMEN

"JAR"

II Cor 4:7: But we have this treasure in Jars of Clay.

Jar in the New Testament, when Jesus turned the water to wine his first miracle, saying here I Am. Water to wine, the Holy Spirit to be poured out on the day of Pentecost, when the jar "JESUS" was Broken to be poured out for All Generations. Our jar now for us always carrying in the body the death of Jesus, so that the life of Jesus may also be manifested in our mortal flesh, our jar, while here on Earth. For us to be poured out in our generation!

IICor 4:7: Jar an earth in vessel, US! but we have this treasure in Jars of Clay. Treasuring the Holy Spirit! Housing the Bread of Life, now the Word of God in us. Be filled with the Holy Spirit until the day of redemption, stay filled. AMEN

"ACTS 10 CORNELIUS HOUSE, TONGUES"

Cornelius a devout man who feared God. I have an interpretation of these tongues. Though they did not speak perhaps a word of any understanding at all, there was something that was understood through what was spoken! They spoke and showed great forgiveness, great joy, happiness, spoke of peace with God now, contentment, great exuberance that could not be understood or spoken with Earthly words, but could be understood with their actions. A smile that did not go away, love for one another not in wanting to depart from each other. The Believers who were circumcised who came with Peter were amazed because the gift of the Holy Spirit was poured on the Gentiles. For they heard them speaking in tongues with without being circumcised! I read no place that their tongues were interpreted. Were they Wrong in Speaking in

Tongues, a gift poured out by God, on the Gentiles when there was no interpretation of what was being said? Some would say so. AMEN

"LUKE 16:19-31 THE RUCH MAN AND LAZARUS"

There was a rich man, I see this rich man as a pastor, teacher of the word. Who feasted sumptuously every day? On to things, the World and the Word of God, Prov 22:9: Whosoever has a bountiful eye will be blessed, for he Shares His Bread with the Poor. At the rich man's gate laid a poor man named Lazarus, who was covered with sores. To me if you had a gate at your house, you had a fence around your property, so I see this man being well-off. Now Lazarus desired to be fed with what crumbs fell from the rich man's table. Lazarus Desire was just to feed of the Richmond wealth in and from God's word, and his Revelation from the spirit of God that Lazarus New the Rich Man had, just some crumbs was his desire. Daily waiting for some crumbs. The rich man's wealth came from not preaching the fullness of the Gospel. The rich man had a large congregation do to preaching only part of the Council of God. Teaching and preaching just to the itching of the people's ears. So, in this he became very rich from the tithes and offerings. But Lazarus New that the rich man had more than he would ever share in church. Therefore Lazarus was Desiring just some of the crumbs from the rich man, If only he would speak them. Lazarus died and carried by the Angels to Abraham's side. The rich man died and was buried. In Hades, he was in torment and lifted up his eyes seen Abraham apply off, and Lazarus at his side. The rich man called out, Father Abraham. The rich man new Abraham and knew him well, calling out Father Abraham have mercy on me and send Lazarus to dip the tip of his finger in water and cool my tongue, or my torment for I am in anguish in these flames. John 7:38 From Lazarus, out of his heart flowed rivers of living waters. John 4:14 But whoever drinks of this water that I will give him will never be thirsty again. The water that I will give him will become in him a spring of water welling up to eternal life. The rich man knew that Lazarus had IT, and wanted this water. Abraham called the Rich Man "Child" capital letter.

Abraham new the rich man as his child. Now let's face it, what is dipping Lazarus finger in water going to do in cooling anyone's torment in hell? NONE! The rich man cried out for just a tip of Lazarus finger dipped in "The Water Of The Word" That My Tongue would be Loosed to Preach the Word of God as I should have preached in the fullness of God's Word if, given the chance again not holding back the true riches found the word of God. Out of your belly rivers of Living Water will flow. having another chance to preach the word of God from what he was holding back, due to the fear of the people.

Isaiah 58:7: Is it not to share your bread with the hungry and bring the homeless, pour into your house, when you see the naked to cover him and not to hide yourself from your own flesh.

Prov 22:9: Whosoever has a bountiful eye will be blessed, for he shares His Bread with the Poor. For there is a great Gap, chasm between you and us. That those who would pass from here to you may not be able, nor any cross from you to us. The rich man said, I beg you Father to send Lazarus to my father's house, for I have five brothers, so that Lazarus may warn them, lease they also come into this place of Torment. So sad that the Rich Man never even told his family. Five brothers, and Mother and Dad. Not preaching the fullness of the gospel and finding out too late. But Abraham said, they have Moses and the Prophets, let them hear them. He said no Father Abraham but if someone goes to them from the dead they will repent. One Rose and came to us from the dead. That is Jesus Christ. there is a great Gulf fixed Between Heaven and Hell and none can pass through to the other side. but there is a bridge to escape hell and it's Jesus Christ he has bridged the gap! For those who believe.

Luke 1:53: He has filled the Hungry with good things and the rich he has sent away empty.

Lazarus' desire was he desired to be fed with the crumbs. I was hungry and you gave me no meat! We're all Beggars Laying at the gate of God's house, what's our Desire? AMEN